# Prepping

*An Essential Survival Guide for DIY Preppers Who Want to Be Self-Reliant When SHTF, Including Tips for Living Off the Grid, Homesteading, and Stockpiling Properly*

© Copyright 2020

All Rights Reserved. No part of this book may be reproduced in any form without permission in writing from the author. Reviewers may quote brief passages in reviews.

Disclaimer: No part of this publication may be reproduced or transmitted in any form or by any means, mechanical or electronic, including photocopying or recording, or by any information storage and retrieval system, or transmitted by email without permission in writing from the publisher.

While all attempts have been made to verify the information provided in this publication, neither the author nor the publisher assumes any responsibility for errors, omissions or contrary interpretations of the subject matter herein.

This book is for entertainment purposes only. The views expressed are those of the author alone, and should not be taken as expert instruction or commands. The reader is responsible for his or her own actions.

Adherence to all applicable laws and regulations, including international, federal, state and local laws governing professional licensing, business practices, advertising and all other aspects of doing business in the US, Canada, UK or any other jurisdiction is the sole responsibility of the purchaser or reader.

Neither the author nor the publisher assumes any responsibility or liability whatsoever on the behalf of the purchaser or reader of these materials. Any perceived slight of any individual or organization is purely unintentional.

# Contents

INTRODUCTION ..................................................................................................1
PART ONE: ESSENTIAL PREPPING.................................................................3
UNDERSTANDING PREPPING........................................................................4
6 MISCONCEPTIONS ABOUT PREPPERS ....................................................6
15 BENEFITS OF PREPPING.............................................................................8
21 THINGS TO KNOW BEFORE BECOMING A PREPPER.....................12
THE BEGINNER'S PREPPING TOOLKIT ...................................................17
PREPPERS TOOLKIT CHECKLIST ..............................................................27
CONSCIOUS STOCKPILING: ITEMS YOU SHOULD NOT SPEND YOUR MONEY ON ........................................................................................................33
31 ESSENTIAL PREPPING SKILLS TO KNOW .........................................38
TOP 15 ROOKIE PREPPER MISTAKES TO AVOID..................................47
PART TWO: OFF-GRID LIVING ....................................................................54
LIVING OFF THE GRID: REASONS AND MISCONCEPTIONS.............55
COMMON MISCONCEPTIONS ABOUT OFF-GRID LIVING.................58
THE REALITIES OF LIVING OFF-GRID.....................................................62
HOMESTEADING 101.......................................................................................66
    Different Types of Homesteading ............................................................... 66
    Basic Homestead Steps ................................................................................. 68
SOLAR ENERGY AND OTHER POWER OPTIONS..................................71

WATER SOURCES, SOLUTIONS, AND SYSTEMS ................................................. 75
    OFF-GRID WATER SOURCES ................................................................. 75
    OFF-GRID WATER UTILIZATION SYSTEMS ............................................. 78
    DETERMINING WHEN WATER DOESN'T NEED FILTERING ..................... 79

THE OFF-GRID BUDGET: HOW MUCH WILL IT COST? ....................... 81
    MAINTENANCE COSTS ........................................................................... 86

PART THREE: SHTF SURVIVAL ............................................................... 88

10 SHTF SCENARIOS: WHAT TO EXPECT AND WHAT TO DO ............. 89

SHTF EVACUATION ..................................................................................... 99

MEDICAL CARE DURING SHTF ................................................................ 104

ADDITIONAL FIRST AID CHECKLIST ...................................................... 112

THE BUG-OUT BAG: SURVIVING SHTF ON THE GO ............................ 114

WILDERNESS SURVIVAL TIPS .................................................................. 118

CONCLUSION ............................................................................................... 122

REFERENCES ................................................................................................ 123

# Introduction

Thank you for choosing *Prepping: An Essential Survival Guide for DIY Preppers Who Want to Be Self-Reliant When SHTF, Including Tips for Living Off the Grid, Homesteading, and Stockpiling Properly* as your preppers guide.

Obviously, you have an interest in learning how to be prepared, and congratulations on taking the right first step.

Prepping is all about being prepared for the worst-case scenario. To begin, look at the example of Super Storm Sandy. Sure, people knew it was coming; they had more than enough warning. They even knew what path it was headed for, and where it would strike first. Were they prepared? No way! Most people affected had lived through bad storms in the past, and that is what they based their prepping on. They didn't prepare for the *absolute worst-case scenario*, and that is what they got.

Most people didn't fully understand how the storm surge would affect them, how the flooding that followed would wreak havoc on their homes and lives. They followed the advice given - to stockpile 72 hours' worth of supplies -, but it wasn't enough. What officials didn't take into account when they drew up their guidelines was the infrastructure - how much it had aged and deteriorated.

And that is why you are here because you don't want to be caught out unprepared. That is what this guide is for – to give you the most up-to-date information to make sure you can survive. And face it – the way the world is going now, anything can happen. The weather is getting more extreme; wars are springing up everywhere, countries like Australia, states like California, even the Amazon, are burning, destroying precious resources and cutting people off, leaving them with no hope of rescue for some time. 72 hours' worth of supplies won't do them any good, and it won't do you any good either.

This book has been written in a way that you will easily understand what to do. It includes step-by-step guides, hands-on tutorials, expert advice, and so much more. There is no fluff, no out-of-date information, and no hard to follow advice. Everything here is simple, sensible, and if you follow it properly, it is pretty easy to implement.

In no time at all, you will be a pro prepper, so dive in now and start this journey of discovery!

# PART ONE: ESSENTIAL PREPPING

# Understanding Prepping

At a fundamental level, prepping is a shortened version of the words "preparation" or "preparing", but its modern use has taken it much further. Now, the word is associated with planning and prepping for disaster scenarios and major catastrophes. It involves basic things, such as stockpiling food, water, medicines, and so on – yet it goes much deeper than that.

To some people, the very idea of stocking up for a large-scale disaster is nothing short of stupid, but the last few years should have taught people differently. The number of weather and war-related disasters is growing, becoming more commonplace than ever before, and it seems now that prepping is the obvious way to go. Who knows when the next disastrous flood will hit? The next out-of-control bushfires? Tornadoes and hurricanes? And, God forbid, who knows when and who will hit that red button?

Being unprepared is to be caught out big style; those who take the time to start prepping now will have a much better chance of survival than those who go through life thinking it will never happen.

Ask yourself this question – *do I have any kind of insurance? Health, life, home?* If you do, that makes you a prepper. Insurance is your preparation for when something goes wrong, and the prepping being talked about here is the same thing. By building up your stockpiles and learning new skills, you are insuring yourself and your family against a future disaster that could lead to society collapsing.

Do you watch the news, read the papers, or listen to the radio? If you do, that means you are well aware of the rise in human-made and natural disasters. Just because they have not happened to you yet doesn't mean they won't, and there is no better way to be ready than to start prepping right now.

The Cold War with Russia was not that long ago, and people still live under the threat of nuclear war every day. Face it - the United States of America doesn't exactly have the best relations with some countries, does it? What about terrorist attacks? Natural disasters? And what if another global pandemic, like the Spanish flu, struck? It could kill billions of people, and the impact on life would be horrendous, not to mention how the economy and society would be affected. How?

Electricity supplies could fail, stores would likely close, and food and water supplies could be heavily depleted. In short, the world as you know it now is in trouble, more than ever before, and everything you have come to take for granted could be gone in seconds. It could happen tomorrow, it could happen next year, in 200 years, or never, and that is the point of prepping - nobody knows when the next disaster will hit; it is just that the preppers are ready for it.

# 6 Misconceptions about Preppers

These are six of the most common misconceptions about preppers:

### 1. Preppers are paranoid conspiracy theorists.

Television can take the blame for this. Many people think preppers are "weirdos", paranoid ones at that. The truth is very different. Preppers are people who simply prefer not to rely on others for their survival should the SHTF. They are actually calm and balanced people who are ensuring they are prepared for anything.

### 2. Preppers are extremists who believe the apocalypse is about to hit.

Not at all. Prepping is nothing to do with zombies or government collapses. It is to do with being prepared for survival in any situation.

### 3. Preppers are isolated.

Sure, some may live out in the wilderness, but your next-door neighbor could be a prepper for all you know. It does not matter where you live; you can learn how to be self-sufficient, build fires, and purify water.

### 4. Preppers are gun fanatics.

It could seem a little extreme when a prepper becomes familiar with self-defense and using guns; however, that doesn't make them a gun fanatic. It is not a bad thing to learn how to protect yourself, so long as your firearms are kept for that reason alone.

### 5. Preppers live in bunkers and are constantly prepping.

Some probably do, but it is not the norm. Preppers are ordinary people, living ordinary lives; it may be a way of life, but it doesn't take over their whole life.

### 6. Preppers are rich.

After all, prepping costs a lot of money, doesn't it? It could do, but it doesn't have to be. You can start prepping now with just a few dollars each month. Most people build up slowly, buying extras here and there. It does not have to cost a fortune and, in many cases, will barely make a difference to the budget you have now.

# 15 Benefits of Prepping

While there are tons of reasons why everyone should start prepping, so many feel it is a waste of their time. So, before you begin prepping or dismiss it out of hand completely, you need to understand the immediate benefits it brings. And these go beyond the main benefit - a better chance of survival during disaster scenarios. So, if you needed any more encouragement to start prepping right now, here are 15 excellent reasons why:

### 1. Save Money

Survival doesn't need to cost a fortune; there are loads of things you can do right now to save money, including:

- Growing your own food
- Making your home safer without forking out for costly alarms
- Make your fitness equipment
- Learn to DIY around the house
- Stock up on dried and canned foods a little at a time

### 2. Better Health

Doing drills, going for hikes and eating better, organic food all lead to a healthier you - being prepared for when the SHTF means getting in shape now. You'll be eating less junk food and consuming more vitamins, minerals, and macro-nutrients to help keep your body healthy too.

### 3. Better Relationships

You've got no choice – planning for doomsday means working together, and prepping can pull even the most broken families back together again. Going for a hike, a camping trip, and even watching survival shows on TV can all help.

### 4. You Become Self-Reliant

Reliance on others is too prevalent in today's society, and although it won't be possible to go entirely off-grid, you can learn self-reliance in many ways – how far you take it is up to you.

### 5. Leadership Skills

If you want to lead your family in survival, you need to become a leader. You must have a vision, learn to encourage others, solve conflicts, and be the leader you need to be. However, you need to learn how to be a leader without coming across overly critical and bossy!

### 6. Learn Responsibility

Becoming a prepper means being responsible, not just for yourself but also for those in your prepper family.

### 7. You Could Make Money

By selling surplus crops to the neighborhood or at the market (by using your survival skills), you learn to help others while earning an income, and even teach others how to survive.

Just be aware of the tax laws surrounding earning extra money and requirements for handling food.

### 8. Never Run Out of Loo Paper Again!

You may be laughing, and it may not be the best reason to begin prepping, but it is true!

### 9. You Won't be so Stressed

Instead of spending your life complaining about what the world is coming to, spend it preparing instead. There won't be such a weight on your shoulders, and you can go through life feeling happier, knowing that, whatever happens, you are prepared for it.

### 10. New Hobbies

Camping, hiking, fishing, learning to build fires, learning to find water sources – the list is endless. Add to that growing your own food, learning new cooking skills, woodwork, DIY, and so on.

### 11. You Could Save a Life

Learning basic first aid and survival medicine is always handy, and you could, one day, use your skills to save a life when no other help is there.

### 12. You won't be So Bored or Lonely

Many people have nothing to do and see no one. Prepping changes all that; not only are you kept busy with your new skills, but you can also join a preppers group and meet new people.

### 13. You Learn Appreciation

Everyone is guilty of forgetting the importance of the small stuff – a bottle of water, an apple from your tree, completing that ten-mile hike. Count your blessings!

### 14. Rediscovering Nature

Do you spend your day divided between the office and your couch at home? Going hiking and camping gets you out there in nature, and that will have positive benefits for you and your life.

### 15. Learning to Negotiate

When you become a prepper, you learn to barter, and that is a form of negotiation. You don't need to wait until the last minute – start bartering now and refine your skills.

Now you know why you should start prepping, read on to learn some other things you need to know.

# 21 Things to Know Before Becoming a Prepper

Most people make mistakes when they start prepping. For most, it is because they rush in, not taking the time to think and plan ahead; for others, it's a lack of decent information. So, here is a list of 21 things you need to know so you do not make the same mistakes, and waste time, energy and money when you don't need to.

### 1. Live Below Your Means - Now

Forget having to use a credit card to purchase all your prepping supplies in one hit - find ways to bring your bills down now and put the money you save to one side.

### 2. Don't Spend Every Penny in Month One

Prepping is a slow and steady business. You might think you need to get that survival item now, but you should look around for deals and wait - patience pays off when you find a better price, or you already have a substitute that will do just as well.

### 3. Start Storing Water

You need water far more than you do food, and a few liters won't get you anywhere. Start storing it now. You don't have to go out and spend a fortune on bottled water; collect your own and store it in clean barrels and collapsible containers in your basement or garage – stored right, it can be kept for long periods.

### 4. Don't Use Old Milk Jugs to Store Water

It might seem like a good idea, but it's doomed from the start. You can never get all the milk residue out of these jugs, and that can lead to your water becoming home to harmful bacteria. Plus, being plastic, the jug will break down over time, and that's a mess you don't want.

### 5. Don't Waste Money on Food That Won't Get Eaten

You might think you found a great deal on a boatload of canned spinach, but does anyone eat it? It's just a waste of precious resources – time, money, and storage space. By all means, look for great deals, but if it doesn't get eaten, don't waste time and money on it.

### 6. Don't Focus Only on Canned Foods

Some people have a strange idea that they should only store canned goods. Wrong – you need a decent variety of foods, including canned, freeze-dried, and dry to ensure you have a decent diet. Otherwise, you run the risk of food boredom setting in. Not only that, canned foods are loaded with sodium, and too much isn't a good thing.

### 7. Make Sure Your Storage Shelves are Sturdy

You might think you got a great deal on those particleboard shelves, but once you start piling goods onto them, they won't last long. Use wire shelving or build your own sturdy wood or metal shelving.

### 8. Don't Store Everything in One Place

One badly timed disaster could wipe out your entire supply of food and other supplies. Keep your food and water separated into several caches, make sure you have a bug-out bag on hand at all times (and one in each vehicle), and keep a few supplies at your bug-out shelter location.

### 9. Prepping is About More Than How Much You Store

It's about learning skills and having the right knowledge to help you survive. You'll need training for some and lots of hands-on experience – at the end of this section, you will find a list of those skills.

### 10. Hygiene and Sanitation Are Important Too

Storing food and water is one thing, but don't forget soap and toilet paper too. Cleanliness is important in avoiding illness – the last thing you want in a survival situation is to fall ill, especially when hospitals will be overrun or, worse, closed altogether.

### 11. Don't Forget Special Needs

There may be people who need wheelchairs, oxygen, insulin, and so on; make sure you include them in your prepping.

### 12. Got Pets? Don't Forget Them

When it comes to a survival situation, you have two choices with pets – abandon them or care for them. Most people will choose the latter, but make sure you make the decision now. Then start stockpiling food and other necessary items for them – and don't forget to factor them into your water calculations.

### 13. Get Family Members On Board

Everyone needs to be in on this; they don't need the same excitement level as you, but they do need to know how to do things and have a certain amount of knowledge. Get them involved from the start.

### 14. Don't Broadcast Your Plans to Everyone

You don't need everyone knowing what you are doing and what you have in stock. If the SHTF, you don't want the whole neighborhood at your door; you can't help your own family and everyone else too. Keep your plans between you, your family, and a few trusted friends.

### 15. Keep in Shape

If you don't, the first day of any disaster scenario is going to leave you exhausted. You'll be hiking about, taking supplies to and from, repairing damage, and it will leave you dead on your feet. It's easier than you think to stay in shape – a power walk for 30 minutes every day will do the trick.

### 16. Don't Assume Guns and Ammo Can Keep You Safe

Yes, you should have guns and plenty of ammo to defend yourself and your family, but you should avoid confrontation where possible. Learn stealth and learn not to draw attention; guns can't keep you safe from others who have them.

### 17. Make a Plan to Get Home

Many people forget that disasters don't wait for them. They can happen when you are anywhere, so make sure you have a plan in place to return home or a safe meeting place for you and your family.

### 18. Never Make Assumptions

Some think that they will need to bug out, and others plan to bug in. The thing is, you have no idea of knowing what's going to happen, so have a plan in place and then have a backup plan. And another if you need it.

### 19. Test Your Tools

Never assume that a tool is going to work when you really need it – test it out. And don't stockpile a dozen of the same tool – if it doesn't work, you may need a different one. Not only that, the more tools you stockpile, the more you have to carry.

### 20. Small Steps

Many DIY projects need a lot of time and education to complete, and patience is the key. Don't rush; take your time, or you will end up frustrated and tired. Many small steps go a long way.

## 21. The World Isn't Going to End Tomorrow

Well, it might, but there's a good chance you'll get a little warning. The problem is some preppers get into the habit of thinking that way and panic; that leads to bad decisions. Always be prepared, but don't forget to enjoy life on the way. Don't lose yourself so much in your doomsday prepping that everything else passes you by and always keep one thing in mind – there is a chance that doomsday won't happen.

# The Beginner's Prepping Toolkit

When it comes to prepping and building up an essential toolkit, there are many things to consider. These are the top ten items and, although most people say you should have enough for 72 hours, you should really be planning for a minimum of two to four weeks.

**Water**

There is a reason this is at the top of the list; as a rule, you can go for at least three weeks eating little to nothing and still survive, but water is a different matter. Depending on conditions, you cannot go without water for more than three or four days, and that is being generous. So, what should you plan for?

You need to store at least one gallon per person per day. If you are prepping for four, aim for a minimum of 28 gallons per week (56 for two weeks and 112 for four). But do keep in mind that you don't just need water for drinking; you need it for cooking and washing too and, if you have pets, factor those into your calculations as well. The best thing to do is to aim for two gallons per day.

You can start by purchasing water at your grocery store, but thinking long term, you should acquire large plastic water storage containers - a mixture of small and large. You will also require water purification tablets and a portable water filter, in case you need to forage for water outside. This is important - drinking dirty water can introduce bacteria and harmful pathogens, and the last thing you need is to be sick on top of trying to survive. You may also use regular, non-scented chlorine bleach, at a rate of two drops per liter, to purify water.

**Food**

The next most important item is food, and again, aim for two to four weeks. You should be starting to stockpile canned foods – soups, meats, fruit, and vegetables, but do make sure they have a decent shelf life and are not dented. You should also be looking at storing dried foods, such as rice, pasta, oatmeal, flour, lentils, and beans. Try to store these in airtight containers, especially the flour, as it can go bad if not stored correctly, and may also attract unwanted rodent and insect attention.

Think about storing sugar, salt, olive or coconut oil, canned cheese and butter, powdered eggs and powdered milk, along with tea and coffee. You can purchase MREs online (Meals Ready-to-Eat), usually from military surplus stores, along with dehydrated and freeze-dried foods. An idea of a list for two weeks' storage is:

- 20 lbs. of beans
- 20 lbs. of rice
- 20 cans of fruit
- 20 cans of vegetables
- 20 cans of meat
- Two large containers of peanut butter
- Two large bags of flour
- One bag of sugar
- One bag of salt*
- One pound of oats
- One gallon of olive or coconut oil

*Don't forget that you can use salt as a preservative for meat and fish, so stockpile as much as you can now.

Obviously, you would only be storing the kinds of foods you and your family eat, and you can change this list to suit your preferences.

Try to aim for a reasonable balance of carbohydrates, fats, and proteins and keep a supply of multivitamins on hand too.

**First Aid**

People take emergency services personnel for granted these days, so much so that most people are unprepared in terms of their own first aid supplies. Should the SHTF, you will need first aid supplies, and there are two ways you can go about it – a basic first aid kit or a full-on medical trauma kit.

At the very least, you and all members of your preppers group should take a first aid course. You should also purchase a survival medicine guide and familiarize yourself with it. If you want, you can purchase survival first aid kits online, or you can make your own. In the checklist at the end of this chapter, a full list of what you need is provided, but as a guide, you will need bandages, Band-Aids, sterile gloves, tweezers, antibiotic and antibacterial creams, and over-the-counter medications.

If you are on prescription medications, you must see your doctor and ensure that you have a decent supply, just in case, and ensure that you have plenty of asthma inhalers on hand if you are asthmatic.

Don't forget; the emergency services are going to be tied up, focusing their efforts on major-impact areas and are not likely to get to you straight away, if at all.

**Sanitation**

Correct sanitation is incredibly important in an SHTF scenario, more so if the electricity and water are out of action. Without it, diseases will soon spread, and that's the last thing you need in this situation.

There are several ways to go here. If your property is on a septic system, usually those properties in outlying or country areas, then you can use your toilet as normal. If there is no running water, you can fill the cistern manually.

If you are not on a septic system, the first thing to do is ensure that the mains sewerage is working – if not, do NOT flush your toilet under any circumstances. Do so, and you risk the sewerage backing up and coming up through your water lines, bathtub, basin, and so on.

In a situation where there is no running water, or you have decamped to your bug-out station, there are a couple of things you can do. A five-gallon bucket double-lined with heavy-duty trash bags may be used as a toilet – you can pop a toilet seat on top if you want. After each use, a generous handful of cat litter or dirt with a little disinfectant spray should be layered on top. When the bag is two-thirds full, cover with litter or dirt and tie it up. Store it out of the way in a sealable container or take it a long way off from where you are living (at least 200 feet), dig a hole, and empty the bag contents into it.

Alternatively, if it is a short-term solution you need, you can dig catholes, again, away from your living area, and make sure they are well-filled in afterward.

Do make sure you have plenty of antibacterial soap, hand sanitizer, and biodegradable toilet paper on hand, as well as a decent supply of wet wipes.

**Cooking**

It's one thing making sure you have a decent supply of food on hand, but, in many cases, you will need a way of cooking it. In most disaster scenarios, the first thing that goes is the electricity supply, and there is every chance it could be off for weeks, even months. Along with that, natural gas supplies may be cut off too.

What you need depends on whether you are bugging in or out. Bug in, and you can go with a propane BBQ (you probably have one in your backyard) or a portable gas stove – for both, you will need a supply of fuel on hand. You could also purchase a supply of disposable BBQs for a quick meal.

If you are bugging out, you can get away with a portable gas stove or building a fire. In both cases, you need quality, durable cooking utensils – you already have these in your home, but do you really want to lug a cast-iron skillet around with you if you have to bug out?

Look for stainless steel pots and pans, tin or stainless steel plates (you can also go for disposable) and quality knives, forks, and spoons. You can purchase kits that take care of all of this, or you can make your own. You must make sure you have a manual can opener, a bottle opener, a decent supply of matches, tin foil, and plastic bags for disposing of leftovers and rubbish.

And don't buy the first or cheapest items you see – do your homework, read reviews, and be sensible about things.

**Power**

The first thing you need is a good flashlight, one for every person in your group. Military or police-grade flashlights are a good option because they have stronger beams, and some have the option of SOS flashing on them. Alongside that is a good supply of batteries, enough for several weeks. Alternatively, purchase rechargeable batteries. You should also keep a couple of wind-up torches on hand as well; they are not that strong, but they don't require batteries and will do in an emergency.

If you are bugging in, then a portable generator is the way to go – you can get a gas-powered one, which means keeping a supply of gasoline on hand, or you can go for a solar-powered generator. You can also purchase battery banks, which can help with short-term charging.

**Cash**

A disaster scenario is when cash truly becomes king – if you have it, you can get almost anything. Start stashing away small bills – aim for about $1,000 as a minimum, although this will depend on how many people are in your survival group. The reason why having small bills is two-fold – first, change is unlikely to be readily available, and second, if you do need to barter, you don't want to be using large notes, and potentially overpaying for things. Plus, it doesn't hurt to let people think you only have a few dollars spare.

Keep your cash reserves safe. First off, don't store it all in the same place. Split it into equal amounts and hide it in different locations – keeping it well hidden, out of sight. Some people choose to bury their cash, wrapping it in several plastic bags first, to keep moisture out. This is fine, so long as you remember where you buried it!

Be aware that, in emergencies, homes are the perfect target for looters – keeping your cash somewhere obvious is a big no-no. Get creative; just make sure you know where it is.

**Communications**

Communication is an important factor in any SHTF scenario. The phone lines are likely to be out of commission, and there is little chance of your mobile phone having any coverage either. You also need to be in touch with others in similar situations and to hear of any news.

What you need, at a minimum, is a two-way radio, preferably one per person in your group or ham radios, and a way of keeping them powered. Typically, these run on batteries, so make sure you have a decent supply. You should also have a radio of some description, a battery-powered or wind-up radio. That way, you can keep up to date with any reports coming in on the situation at hand and what, if any, emergency help is on the way.

It is worth noting that, although it is illegal to broadcast on ham radios, it has been deemed legal in the case of an emergency.

**Mobility**

Mobility is also an important consideration. If you are in a position to leave your home and evacuate somewhere safe, then you should ensure that you have sufficient fuel to get you away. If the situation is such that traveling simply isn't an option, you have to decide whether to bug in or bug out. In most cases, bugging in won't be an option –

electricity, water, and gas lines will be out of commission, and if the disaster is such that your home has been damaged, you will need to get out.

In that case, you need your bug-out bag, and that, as a minimum, should contain emergency shelter, water, food, and security. In part three of this guide, there is more detail on the bugout bag, but for now, here is an idea of what you should have in it – and each person should have one:

- Tent
- Sleeping bag
- Space blanket
- Water bottle or bladder
- Portable filter
- Food rations
- Gloves
- Jacket
- One change of clothes
- Warm headgear
- Matches
- Flashlight
- Headlamp
- Basic first aid kit
- Map of the area
- Compass
- Mini shovel
- Ax/hatchet
- Paracord
- Multi-tool
- Knife
- Pepper spray
- Charger – solar or battery

- Whistle
- Goggles
- Copies of your important documents
- Passport
- Titles and contracts
- Address book
- Family disaster plan
- At least $500 cash – small bills
- Prescription medication
- Small mirror

**Self-Defense**

Bugging in or bugging out, self-defense is vital. In disaster scenarios, anything can happen, and you need to bear in mind that most people will only be prepared for a couple of days – after all, FEMA (Federal Emergency Management Agency) recommends you prepare for just 72 hours. Everyone knows that most disaster situations continue long after this, and so long-term planning is crucial.

When people get desperate, they will do anything to survive, and if that means attacking you to get what you have, they will. And they won't think twice about hurting you either. If you are bugging in, there are certain things you can do to ensure a certain level of safety – make sure you have high fencing all around the property, set up obstacles to slow down would-be attackers, make sure all your windows and doors are bolted shut, and so on. However, in the event that someone makes it past all that, or you are bugging out, you need to consider how you will defend yourself.

You should keep weapons on hand. At the very least, have stun guns and/or Tasers. Stun guns require that you have direct contact with your attacker, while Tasers can be fired from a distance – while most Tasers don't have a strong enough shock capacity to need a permit, you must check regulations in your area. Having said that, in a real apocalypse-type scenario, not many people will be worried about regulations!

Pepper spray is one of the best defense weapons – it is easy to conceal, light, and simple to use. Knives are easily concealed, but again, unless you are a professional knife thrower, you need to be up close and personal with your attacker.

And then there are guns. Not everyone is comfortable carrying and using a firearm, but sometimes the situation may warrant it. Consider keeping a 12-gauge shotgun on hand, and a hand pistol, along with plenty of ammunition. Do make sure you know how to use one; there are plenty of gun ranges you can attend for training.

Martial arts may be something some people laugh at, but self-defense is exactly what the martial arts are all about. One particularly good one to consider learning is Krav Maga, but you could just as easily opt for judo, Taekwondo, or karate – each serves its purpose well.

## OPSEC

This comes under self-defense, but it is best discussed separately. OPSEC stands for Operations Security, and it really means to keep things on a need to know basis. In other words, don't go blabbing your plans to all and sundry. Don't let everyone know what stores you have in place because, when the SHTF and people run out of supplies, they'll be at your door, looking to share what you spent precious time and money on.

However, there is another school of thought that you don't have to keep things entirely secret. There is no harm in getting all your neighbors together, explaining what a prepper is, and why they should get in on the act right now. More people need to be educated on what the prepper lifestyle is all about, but what you don't need to do is tell them where you keep your food, your money, what weapons you have stockpiled, where your bug-out location is, and so on.

The thing is, even if you don't tell anyone, or keep it purely within your family, others will soon notice that something is going on. For example, you head to the grocery store, and they have 5lb. bags of beans and rice on special offer or the flour is "buy one, get one free". These are on your list, so it makes good sense to buy them at the special price, but do you really think that no one will notice that you have 6 lbs. of flour and 20 lbs. each of rice and beans? Do you think nobody will notice when the UPS van starts delivering numerous boxes to your door?

Keep things as secret as you need to, but keep it real too.

# Preppers Toolkit Checklist

You will not necessarily require everything on this list – much of it will depend on the situation at hand. Use your head, keep things sensible, and remember: You may have to travel on foot to get away from your area; do you really want to be carrying half a ton of stuff for miles?

**Water**

- A minimum of one gallon per person per day, preferably more
- Portable water filters
- Purification tablets
- Standard chlorine bleach (unscented), 8.25% sodium hypochlorite
- A way of boiling water – gas stove and gas canisters, matches

**Food**

These are absolute minimum amounts for two weeks:

- 20 lbs. of rice
- 20 lbs. of beans
- 20 cans of vegetables
- 20 cans of fruit
- 20 cans of meat

- Two bags of flour
- One bag of sugar
- One bag of salt
- One pound of oats
- One gallon of olive or coconut oil

**Other foods:**

- Freeze-dried foods
- Dehydrated foods
- Coffee
- Tea
- Powdered milk
- Powdered eggs
- Canned cheese
- Canned butter
- Instant potatoes
- Pasta
- Canned or packet soups

**First Aid**

- First aid case/bag – waterproof, lightweight
- Survival medicine/first aid handbook
- Tweezers
- Infrared forehead thermometers
- Antibacterial Q-tips
- Large trauma shears
- Surgical grade toenail clippers
- Scalpel plus spare blades
- Stethoscope
- Blisters plasters
- Band-Aids – various sizes
- Sterile gloves

- Sterile gauze pads – various sizes
- Alcohol wipes
- Bandages – various sizes
- Triangular bandages
- CPR pocket mask
- Steri-Strips (or equivalent)
- Moldable foam split
- Iodine
- Tourniquet
- Sunblock
- Bug repellent
- Burn cream/gel
- Medications and ointments
- Antibiotic cream
- Hydrocortisone
- Antifungal cream
- Antibacterial soap
- Ibuprofen
- Paracetamol
- Tylenol
- Sudafed (or equivalent)
- Antihistamine cream and tablets
- Imodium (or equivalent)
- Throat lozenges
- Oral rehydration
- Prescription medications
- Asthma inhalers
- Multivitamins

**Sanitation**

- Five-gallon bucket

- Heavy-duty trash bags
- Sealable container
- Cat litter
- Disinfectant spray
- Antibacterial soap
- Hand sanitizer
- Wet wipes
- Biodegradable toilet paper

**Cooking**

- Portable gas/propane stove
- Gas/propane
- Stainless steel pots and pans
- Cooking utensils – knives, forks, spoons, etc.
- Plates (tin/stainless steel/disposable)
- Disposable BBQs
- Can opener (manual)
- Bottle opener
- Trash bags
- Matches
- Wood
- Power
- Flashlights – one per person
- Plenty of spare batteries – standard and/or rechargeable
- Power/battery bank
- Portable generator – solar or gasoline
- Gasoline – if choosing a gas-powered generator
- Wind-up flashlights

**Cash**

- A minimum of $1,000 in small bills

- Plastic bags/storage containers

**Communications**

- Two-way or ham radio – one each
- Spare batteries
- Battery or wind-up radio

**Mobility**

- Tent
- Sleeping bag
- Space blanket
- Water bottle or bladder
- Portable filter
- Food rations
- Gloves
- Jacket
- One change of clothes
- Warm headgear
- Matches
- Flashlight
- Headlamp
- Basic first aid kit
- Map of the area
- Compass
- Mini shovel
- Ax/hatchet
- Paracord
- Multi-tool
- Knife
- Pepper spray
- Charger – solar or battery
- Whistle

- Goggles
- Copies of your important documents
- Passport
- Titles and contracts
- Address book
- Family disaster plan
- At least $500 cash – small bills
- Prescription medication
- Small mirror

**Self-Defense**

- Shotgun
- hand pistol
- Ammunition
- Pepper spray
- Knife
- Taser
- Stun gun

# Conscious Stockpiling: Items You Should NOT Spend Your Money on

For some people, those who have plenty of cash, prepping is easy, but for those with little spare income every month, it is hard. Most people have been in this situation before, and many still are. Everyone knows that, when bad times happen, they have to start cutting back on what they do, and prepping is one of those things - many preppers have had to put a stop to it and start living off their accumulated stores, just to survive. Having that stock of food can be a real godsend, but it won't last forever, and somewhere along the line, you have to start again.

The first thing to get into your mind is that prepping doesn't need to be expensive, and there are plenty of ways that you can prep for free; you just have to change your mindset to one that says you should never waste what can be used later. This isn't always easy, but drawing up a proper plan, does make it easier.

### Survival Food

One thing you can do is opt to use every last scrap of food, saving you money on your food budget. The trouble is that most people don't want to eat the same thing day after day, but you don't have to. Food leftovers are free food for your survival stores, and you can make this work in several ways:

- **Dehydrate leftover beans, pasta, and rice**

Most people make too much, and most throw away what they don't eat. Stop. Dehydrate them, and when you really need a meal, all you need to do is rehydrate them for a few minutes in boiling water. Once dehydrated, vacuum pack the food for easier storage.

- **Canned meat and meat dishes**

Did you cook too much chili or Bolognese? Pressure can it following the correct canning process. If you don't have enough for that, store it in your freezer until you do and then can the whole lot.

- **Dehydrate bread**

If you have leftover bread, rather than throw it out, dehydrate it and turn it into an instant stuffing mix (check the internet; there are plenty of different recipes) or even into breadcrumbs for breading fish, meat, etc.

- **Get free food**

It can be done. All you need to do is save and stack your coupons. You'll get plenty of freebies and, in some cases, they may even pay you to take them home. Don't go overboard with this; just pick the stuff that you can store long term. And there are couponing classes you can attend to learn how to do it.

- **Free fruit**

Most yards have fruit trees, and for the most part, much of it is left to rot. Don't be afraid to ask if you can have some. Offer to pay for it, but most of the time, people will tell you to take as much as you want. What then? Make it into jams and jellies, can it, or even dehydrate it.

- **Free food samples**

A large number of food storage organizations will happily send out free samples of their products in the hopes that you will order more. Even if you don't buy any more, the free samples will go nicely in your bug-out bag or emergency food kit.

- **Keep your condiment packs**

When you order takeout or head to a fast-food restaurant, grab some condiment packs. These fit nicely into your food kits, but be aware; they don't last all that long, so plan on replacing them yearly.

- **Save drink bottles for water**

Don't waste money buying bottled water. Simply keep all your drink bottles, wash them thoroughly, and fill them from the tap. The only thing this doesn't apply to is milk containers as milk residue taints the water.

### Household and Garden Survival

Couponing can pay off here too; save coupons for toiletries, toilet paper, toothbrushes, toothpaste, razors, and other household items – you can get an awful lot of these for free. And when you visit the dentist, ask for free samples.

- **Save your seeds**

Be it free seeds in magazines or seeds from plants you grow, vacuum pack them, and save them in a cool, dark cupboard. That way, you can grow your own vegetables when the need arises.

- **Grown new plants from vegetable roots**

When you buy vegetables or even grow them in your garden, you can regrow them from the roots. Celery, lettuce, onions, even pineapples, and so many other vegetables and fruits may be regrown in this way. Chop off the root end and suspend it in water until you see the roots growing and/or shoots from the top. Then simply plant it in soil and watch it grow. If you stagger your growing, you can have an almost never-ending cycle of free food.

- **Free plants**

Check with your neighbors to see if you can have cuttings or roots from their herbs, and other edibles. They may even give you entire plants if you are lucky. And then just plant them and enjoy the fruits of your labor. If you have an excess of some plants, you can share those or even swap with neighbors.

- **Free mulch and compost**

Many tree trimmers or your county will often have free mulch and compost, but be careful with it – it may be full of insects and pests, not something you want to introduce to your garden!

- **Collect pine cones**

They make great fire starters and burn very hot and quickly. Start collecting them in fall when they are on the ground and store them somewhere cool and dry.

- **Free sandbags**

If there is any chance of flooding, your county may hand out free sandbags. You do need to be quick to get them because they tend to go fast, but they make a great addition to your prepping, especially for the hurricane season.

### Shelving and Furniture

Keep your eye on Craigslist, freecycle lists, or for items that people leave outside, free to a good home. You might be surprised at what you can find for free.

### Preppers Supplies

- **Free buckets**

You can get these from commercial kitchens; some charge a tiny amount, but on the whole, if you check by their dumpsters, you'll find them for free. Do ask them, but usually, they will tell you to take them away. You can also ask at bakeries, fast-food restaurants, and delis too.

- **Popcorn tins**

These aren't in such wide supply now, but if you can get hold of the three or five-gallon size tins, they make great storage containers. They are rat/mouse-proof, and you can store quite a bit of packaged food in them.

- **Free batteries, tarps, flashlights, etc.**

Some stores offer these for free with no purchase needed, but more often than not, you will need to buy something else. It's still a free item that you would otherwise have to pay for, though, so you are saving money.

- **Free Samples**

Some of these have already been mentioned, but do keep your eye out for internet ads that offer freebies, such as small flashlights, multi-purpose tools, paracord bracelets, etc., especially on survival websites. And provide a company with an honest review of a product they sell, and you may get a coupon for a freebie as a way of saying thanks – this tends to work better with the large manufacturers.

- **Free information and Books**

Check out the kindle app store for free books. They won't be as detailed as this guide, but you can pick up short survival cookbooks, first aid books, and so on.

These may all seem like small things, but the value soon adds up. There is no requirement to have money in the bank to begin prepping, and you can get so much for free if you know where to look and stop wasting so much at home. Your garden is a great source of free food, too; it doesn't take much to get a few vegetables growing.

# 31 Essential Prepping Skills to Know

Every prepper and survivalist will have their own priority list of skills to learn, alongside their tasks and gear. Being a prepper really isn't easy, but learning the skills won't just stand you in good stead when it comes to a survival situation; they can also help you after the disaster.

No prepper learns just one skill; you really do need to be a jack of all trades. You must be as prepared as you possibly can be for whatever emergency arises. And face it – no one knows when it might happen, so now is as good a time as any to learn your skills.

So many people think prepping is all about stockpiling food and gear, and while that is a big part of it, it's also about what you know and what you can do.

**Beneficial Prepper Skills**

There are many skills that you should know, but while every member of your prepper family should have some knowledge about all skills, it is OK to delegate so that each of you learns some useful skills.

**Bushcraft**

Bushcraft is an ancient art that uses natural resources to survive in the wilderness. It isn't one skill; it's a group of skills that encompass:

### 1. Foraging for food

This includes knowing what plants you and can't eat, how to cook over a campfire, and how to harvest efficiently without destroying a resource completely. Many plants will regrow if you take a little care, rather than hauling them up by the roots - that's a sustainable source of food. You need to understand what mushrooms you can and can't eat and how to cook them.

### 2. Hunting/trapping/fishing

Learn how to track and stalk animals for food, how to build a snare and where the best places are to set them. Learn how to hide your scent - remember: Animals have a much better hearing and sense of smell than humans do; they'll know you are there long before you see them. You need to be able to ties knots, make cordage, and importantly, learn how to prepare and cook what you catch. You must also learn how to build and use weapons, such as slingshots and a bow and arrow, all of which can be made from natural resources. When times get desperate, everyone with a weapon will be after the same food sources, and those who prep properly will know exactly what's in their area and know how to catch and preserve it. Another useful skill in this area is fishing - most places have a body of water where some fish are available, and knowing how to catch them and preserve your catch is a vital survival skill.

### 3. Finding and gathering water

Water sources are more prevalent than you realize; you just need to learn where to look for them. Once you've found your water source, learn how to filter and purify it, so it is drinkable, and if you don't have one, learn how to make a container to collect and carry water in.

### 4. Building a shelter

This is important; you won't survive long out in the elements, no matter how well prepared you are. You must learn how to fell a tree for materials, baton branches, and find other materials you need to construct your shelter. For example, bark and grass can be thatched or woven to make a roof. You must also learn what materials you can use to both insulate and waterproof your new home.

### 5. Building a fire

Another very important factor for survival is knowing how to build a fire. Learn the best woods for quick burning and longer burning times, what constitutes tinder, how to build a fire-starting device, such as a fire plow or a bow drill, and how to build a firepit. You should also learn to make charcoal.

### 6. Navigation

Learning to use a compass or even a watch for navigation is a vital skill, but you should also learn to use other methods, such as the sun, stars, and even landmarks.

There are plenty of courses you can take to learn all this, along with videos and other resources.

**Backpacking and Camping**

Two very important skills:

### 7. Backpacking

Not only is backpacking fun, but it's also a great way of getting in shape and learning how to traverse different terrains carrying your survival gear. You'll learn how to carry your bug-out bag properly – the weight should be on your hips, not on your shoulders. You'll learn how to keep the ticks, mosquitoes, and other insects away, avoid injuries to your legs and feet, and how to work together as a group.

### 8. Camping

Camping is a no-brainer really, and it's much easier to learn than backpacking because you don't need to hike out anywhere. You can learn how to camp in your backyard, and you should already have your camping equipment ready – get out there and start practicing. Stocking up on freeze-dried and dehydrated foods for your camping trips means your prepping skills are not going to waste – you get to find out which ones you like and don't like before you fork out for bulk amounts.

## Food Survival

There are several factors here:

### 9. Baking bread

You should learn how to bake a basic bread over a campfire by hand - no bread maker here! You'll also learn to make biscuits, flatbread, tortillas, and other nice bread. Invest in a grain mill if you are bugging in, and learn to mill your own flour.

### 10. Bee-keeping

If you are bugging in, learn how to keep bees and extract the honey for food and the wax for making candles. You should also learn how to brew your own beer, not just for your own consumption but for bartering purposes too.

### 11. Learn to make butter and cheese

If you have livestock, such as a cow, learn how to churn your own butter. It's hard work, but incredibly satisfying when you get to taste your own butter. And you can also make cheese from the milk of cows, sheep, and goats - but remember to wax it to preserve it for longer.

### 12. Preserving food

You must learn how to can your own food too. Fruits, vegetables, even meat may be canned, and it's even better if you grow and raise your own food. Not only do they make for good meals, but you can also use canned foods for bartering.

Charcuterie is a great skill to learn, the art of curing, smoking, drying, and salting meat and fish. You should also learn how to properly dehydrate food, especially if you don't have the luxury of a dehydrator at your disposal. This is one of the best ways of preserving food, but be aware that it is labor-intensive. Learning to freeze-dry is a better method.

### 13. Entomology

Grimace, if you want, but learning how to tell the difference between poisonous and edible insects is a great survival skill to learn. For example, crickets are full of fats, protein, and vitamins, vital for energy and health while in the wilderness. As a rule, the bright-colored bugs tend to be poisonous and should be avoided.

**Homesteading Skills**

Homesteading is all about self-sufficiency and encompasses many different skills:

### 14. Keep chickens

It's dead fashionable these days to have a few chickens in your yard, and it's a great way of prepping. First, you get a good supply of eggs that you can use for cooking – you can even freeze-dry them for future use. Chickens are natural gardeners too, keeping your land free of insects and producing fertilizer, and, as a last resort, they are a good source of food.

### 15. Learn to compost

There is a right and wrong way to do it; if you don't know how to do it and what you can and can't compost, you are at risk of illness. And it's important to know how to compost human waste too.

### 16. Gardening and saving seeds

Gardening is a great skill to learn; not only is it physical exercise, but it also gets you out in the fresh air, and you can grow your own vegetables and fruits. You can grow as little or as much as you want – the more you grow, the more you have to preserve for the future, and gardening is quite simple once you get the hang of it, and it's not expensive. You should also learn to harvest seeds from your plants; that way, you can keep your crops going for as long as you need. And some seeds are a great source of food, such as pumpkin and sunflower seeds.

Another great tip is to build yourself a walipini. This is an underground greenhouse, where, built right, you can grow vegetables and fruits all year around. Make it big enough, and you also have your very own storage room, out of the elements and out of sight. There are also cases of people enlarging them so they can live in them when the need arises.

### 17. Learn to knit, sew and crochet

Socks won't darn themselves, and you may not have the option of purchasing new clothing. As such, it's important that you keep what you have repaired and is fit to wear. You can also learn to make new clothes, including socks and slippers.

### 18. Raise livestock

Apart from chickens, there are other animals you can raise for resources. You don't need to get a cow, and not everyone has the room for one. Instead, consider these:

- **Rabbits** – these take a lot of care, and you must keep the buck and doe apart unless you are breeding them. These give you a great source of protein-rich meat and fur for clothing.
- **Goats** – these are more practical and a bit easier to keep than rabbits and provide multiple benefits: highly nutritional meat, a way of keeping your land clear (they can create a fire break around your property), milk (from which you can make cheese, soap, and yogurt), hide, which you can tan into leather, hair for making into mohair, and lastly, dung (you can use this for compost when it's fresh or as fire fuel when it's dried).

Any of these animals can be a lifesaver in terms of food and useful materials.

### 19. Making soap

Learning to make soap can save you a fortune in the long run, especially if you have goat's milk on hand. You can even make soap from ash!

### 20. Shoemaking

One of the lost arts, shoemaking is a very important skill to learn and could save you money – as well as preventing you from having bad feet.

## First Aid Skills

There are a couple of main points here:

### 21. Basic first aid

Taking a basic first aid course is a must – it can be the difference between life and death when there is no access to medical help. You can take things further and go on to learn emergency medical technician skills.

### 22. Herbal healing

One more thing you can do is learn herbal healing – there are plenty of plants and herbs that can be used as medicine.

## Communication skills

One of the most important skills to learn is communication, not just between your prepper family members but others around you too.

### 23. HAM Radio

Communication is key to knowing about food and water supplies, what condition other areas are in, and in finding out the latest disaster status. Although you need a license to operate one and it isn't the cheapest equipment, it is a vital skill to learn. Plus, although illegal to broadcast, in a disaster situation, you can do it.

### 24. Morse code

This is an interesting one but a potential lifesaver when all communications are down. With a series of simple dashes and dots, you can communicate just about anything – on paper, visually, via sound, via body language, using flashlights, and much more.

### Other Useful Skills

While the above are vital skills, there are other important ones you should learn too:

#### 25. Self-defense

Yes, you could use a gun, but there are other less lethal ways to protect you and your family. You could learn any one of several martial arts, and although they can be lethal, they don't have to be. They do ensure your self-confidence, and they can prove to potential attackers that you mean business.

#### 26. Swimming

Not everyone can swim, but you should learn. The planet is 75 percent water, and there is a good chance that you will need to cross some at some point. You must know how to swim fully dressed, swim underwater, and get yourself out of trouble in the water.

#### 27. Welding

This is a great skill that anyone can learn how to do. It can prove invaluable for repairing vehicles, making weapons, and even creating your own source of energy.

#### 28. Couponing

Learning how to coupon efficiently can result in a ton of savings, and even freebies that can help you in your prepping. Believe it or not, you can even take courses on how to do it.

#### 29. Paracord

Paracord is one of the most popular prepper materials and has a multitude of uses. It's high strength and can be used for lashing together shelters, make-shift furniture, belts, braces, keychain bombs, and many other things. This is one skill you will never regret learning.

### 30. Whittling

Learning to whittle can help you produce useful items, including a bow and arrow, a slingshot, games to keep the kids occupied, and so on. And you can use the wood shavings to help you light a fire.

### 31. Bartering

A very important skill to learn is how to barter with very little, trading up as you go. Or using your excess to barter between neighbors, using the money you salted away, and so on. You can barter with just about anything, but one tip is this: Never let on how much you have. People get easily jealous, and that leads to trouble, especially in desperate times.

There are loads of skills you should learn as part of your prepping for when the SHTF and these are the most important and useful.

# Top 15 Rookie Prepper Mistakes to Avoid

As mentioned, prepping isn't easy to do, and as a beginner, you are likely to make many mistakes. You can scare yourself to death reading everything you find on the internet about prepping, especially when people talk about things that went wrong. However, proper preparation and attention to detail mitigate most risks – you cannot account for everything, but you can certainly reduce the potential for things to go wrong.

To that end, here are the top 15 mistakes that you should avoid making:

### 1. Keep Your Mouth Shut! Do Not Tell Others About Your Emergency Shelter

Have you ever watched "Shelter Skelter", an old *The Twilight Zone* episode? Find it on YouTube and watch it – it will tell you why you should keep your mouth shut. In short, a man at a party shoots his mouth off about his emergency shelter. Then, when the emergency sirens go off, every one of his neighbors turns up at his door, smashing the shelter door off. It turns out that it was a false alarm, but if it happened to you and the cause was an atomic blast, you would have received a huge dose of radiation.

The only people you should tell are those that you trust 100 percent and that you want joining you in your shelter should the need arise. The only other people you can talk to it about are other preppers if you have a community near your home. Other than that, keep it zipped and tell no one else.

Desperate people are the most dangerous, and the last thing you need is desperate people trying to get into your last safe place.

### 2. Not Doing Your Disaster Scenario Homework

Some disasters are common in certain areas, and the biggest mistake you can make is not prepping for what is common in your area. It's fine if you've prepped for all potential scenarios, but if you, for example, prep for the worst case, such as nuclear fallout, and not for tornadoes that are common in your area, then you're going to be out of luck when the next one hits.

Say that your area is prone to severe flooding every ten years or so. You might think that ten years is a long time and the last one only happened two years ago - you've got plenty of time, right? Wrong. With global warming and the crazy weather patterns of late, another flood could happen at any time. And if you're not prepared for it, you could be in serious trouble.

Obviously, you don't want an underground shelter in a flood scenario - you will lose the lot. And what if you live in a hurricane-prone area? You may not have to leave your home, but you should be prepared for water, gas, and electricity supplies to fail, at least for a few days. You also need to be prepared for the temperatures - a disaster can strike at any time, be it the height of summer and or in the depths of a frozen winter.

### 3. Not Staying in Shape

As a prepper, you need to be ready for anything, and that means staying in shape. You cannot possibly protect yourself, your family, and your property if you can't even make it up one flight of stairs without collapsing at the top.

You live in a fast, busy world, and there isn't always enough time to work out. And then there's the expense of a gym membership to consider. Well, you don't have to join a gym to get in shape. Start working out at home instead. There are plenty of exercises you can do in just five minutes at home. And if you take public transport to work, get off at an earlier stop and walk the rest of the way. Take the stairs, not the escalator or elevator; go for a half-hour walk at lunchtime. So many things you can do, and it all adds up to a fitter, more prepared you. And if your family needs to get in shape too, head out for bike rides and hikes on the weekends.

### 4. You Don't Have any Training or Survival Skills

It's all very well splashing out on expensive survival gadgets and spending a fortune on prepping - which you don't have to do -, but you also need to learn the necessary skills to use such gadgets to the best effect. Buy whatever you think will work, but take the time to learn how to use it in the event of an SHTF scenario.

Think about it; you get caught out in a crisis, you don't have your bug-out bag with you or any weapons for self-defense. Or you do, and you don't know how to use them. What then? You could rely on yourself to a certain extent, but without survival skills and training, you won't last long in the face of danger.

Provided you are in good shape, learned self-defense, and have a variety of survival skills under your belt, you have a much better chance of surviving pretty much any disaster situation. You don't have to be Bear Grylls, but you do need some skills.

### 5. Not Choosing the Right Foods for Long-term Storage

You might think any old dried or canned food will do, and there are some strange items that you might see on survival videos that really are not suitable items to stockpile. Take Ramen noodles or Ramen soups - there is more nutrition in a cardboard box! They are not healthy and are full of salt, and unless you have several liters of water spare to wash it down - which you won't have -, you won't last long living on them. Plus, they contain no protein and no other nutritional value.

You must check the labels on the food you store. Too many people pack their kits full of high-sodium snacks – while it is nice to have the odd treat, that's not what this is about. Concentrate on ensuring you store foods with a balance of protein, fat, and carbohydrate – these are the essential macronutrients for health. Having a few salty snacks on hand is fine, but don't go overboard – be sure to do your research before you buy emergency food stores on the internet.

### 6. You Have Too Many Small Pets

This could be a controversial point. Most people prep for natural disasters and smaller-scale disasters, those that could leave them with no power or water for days or longer, and in these cases, a couple of smaller animals is fine. If you are one of those that believes the apocalypse is just around the corner, though, and you must have an animal, get a bigger one.

Large dogs can help protect you when you are trying to survive, while smaller animals will drag you down.

### 7. Forgetting to Have Something to Exercise Your Mind

Whether you bug in or bug out, you need to have something to keep your mind ticking over. While food and water are important for survival, don't neglect your mind. Put some books in your stockpile, a mixture of genres, and don't forget to include a few survival books too – these will be of great benefit in an SHTF scenario. Put away books on creating a garden, food preservation, first aid skills, and anything else you can think of that will help in a desperate situation.

You should also store a few board games, packs of cards, puzzle books, and other fun things that will keep you occupied and stop your brain, turning to mush.

### 8. You Don't Have Fitness Gear in Your Emergency Shelter

This doesn't refer to "the big stuff", like running machines and so on, but you should have some kind of exercise equipment. Not only will it keep your fitness levels up, but research also shows that exercise can stop you from becoming depressed.

All you need is a few dumbbells, a set of resistance bands, and any other small fitness equipment you can think of. That type of gear can even go with you if you need to bug out.

### 9. You Have Far Too Much Reliance on Electronics

How many prepper videos have you seen where people bury items and then mark them on their GPS? You might think that's a great idea, but what happens if the grid goes down? What happens if a massive electromagnetic pulse (EMP) bursts in your area? That's right, your GPS won't work, and you won't find where you buried your gear.

Do things the old-fashioned way – learn how to read and use a map. People do still use them; not everyone relies on a GPS to get them where they need to go. Invest in a map showing your area and a bit wider out if necessary. You can also invest in a map book, showing the whole country. That way, you can get where you need to go without relying on a GPS.

You should also learn to navigate by the sun and stars – it's not as hard as you think. You can also purchase a small Faraday cage or Faraday bag that will keep your electronics safe in the event of an EMP.

### 10. You Spend Far Too Much on Survival Gadgets

This is another major mistake by prepper beginners. You start surfing the Net, looking for survival gear, and you get sidetracked by expensive, unnecessary gadgets. How many variations of a knife have you seen? How many different axes or flashlights? At the end of the ay, you should keep it simple. Buy only what you really need and leave the gadgets to someone else. Set yourself a monthly budget and don't go over it.

## 11. You Don't Monitor Expiry Dates

You should always have water purification tablets on hand and two types of food storage – near future and far future. For the latter, make sure you check expiry dates and rotate your stock regularly. When you buy items, stick an expiry label on it and have things stored in order of their date – this also applies to your water containers, as water will go bad if not stored properly or it gets contaminated in some way. Your water purification tablets will help if your water goes green, so make sure you have plenty of them and that they are always in date.

## 12. Failing to Stay Organized

This is, without a doubt, one of the worst mistakes you can make. It's one thing to ensure you have adequate food stock, but storing it in a room and then forgetting about it is not good practice – by the time you need it, it may no longer be edible.

You should also plan for the eventuality that you may need to evacuate – not just your home but your town or city. Make sure you have a bug-out plan in place that gives you a fast, safe way out, avoiding huge traffic tailbacks.

## 13. You Don't Have Enough Water

Most preppers aim for 72 hours' worth of food, but water is a different matter. You might think a couple of cases will do the trick, but it won't. You have to consider at least two liters of water per person per day for drinking, more if the temperatures are high. Then factor in cooking and washing, and you can see it starts to add up. The minimum is a gallon per person per day – bear in mind that you can go for three weeks without food but only three days with no water – make it your top priority.

## 14. Planning to Bug Out and Not Bug In

Many preppers focus on scenarios where they have to evacuate their homes and travel into the woods to bug out. But not all scenarios require that; when earthquakes or hurricanes strike, the best place you can be is in your basement, safe at home.

At the end of the day, bugging in is always going to be better than bugging out, but few preppers even consider it and don't bother making a plan. Clearly, you need to focus on a bug-out plan because the implications are more serious, but never neglect a plan to stay at home for a few days.

## 15. Keeping Your Prepping Gear Together in One Place

Another common rookie mistake is storing everything in the same place. It might seem sensible, but really, it isn't. For example, say that you store everything in your garage. When a hurricane hits, your garage is the weakest point - what if you can't get into it to get all your gear out? Spread your gear around your home, so at least some of it is accessible should the need arise. You could even consider a rented storage locker for some stuff - that way, if you are out and can't get back to your home, you at least have access to something you can use.

That brings you to the end of Part One of this SHTF prepping guide; in the next part, you will look at homesteading.

# PART TWO: OFF-GRID LIVING

# Living Off the Grid: Reasons and Misconceptions

Right now, there are almost two billion people living off-grid in the world, not all of them by their own choice. In the United States alone, more than 200,000 families have made the leap, and that number is growing by the year. Much of that is down to more people becoming conscious of the environment, and some of it is down to preppers preparing for an SHTF scenario – a real possibility, given current events in the world, both human-made and natural.

So, what is off-grid living? The simple way to define it is living in a way that you do not rely on utilities, like water, electricity, sewers, gas, and so on, provided by public services. It means that you generate and provide everything yourself, and there are plenty of ways to do it. You don't have to go totally off-grid right from the start, either. You can start small and build up until you are self-sufficient.

Preppers for SHTF scenarios are doing this right now. Some purchase specific properties, while others are gradually turning their properties into self-sufficient ones. And this is all being done alongside stockpiling food and other survival gear.

### Reasons for Going Off-Grid

Now, for the prepper, there are two major scenarios you need to prep for in terms of off-grid living – the hurricane/flood/tornado, etc., that knocks your utilities out for several days, or an end-of-the-world, apocalypse scenario, where everything is gone long term, possibly forever.

For others, the choice to go off-grid is entirely conscious, a decision made for many different reasons.

1. **Self-sufficiency** – that's what living off-grid is all about, not depending on external resources because you can make your own. For the prepper, this is important as it removes your reliance on a system that might collapse at any given moment.

2. **Sustainability** – it's all about living a sustainable life, not draining already stretched resources. You will produce more than consume, not only providing for your family but helping your community too.

3. **Renewable energy** – renewable energy makes all the sense in the world, and it really is common sense against using sources that are not renewable, at least not at the speed that people use them.

4. **It's responsible** – in terms of the environment, at any rate, and everyone has to bear the responsibility to make the world better. The more people who choose to go off-grid, the better people can make the environment, and the more chance there is that their children and grandchildren will have a decent world to live in.

5. **It's practical** – pretty much all, or at least most, of people's resources are reused and recycled, getting the maximum amount of use out of them.

6. **A smaller carbon footprint** – living off-grid means fewer resources are used, and less waste is produced.

7. **Healthy lifestyle** – not only are you more active, but you tend to eat a healthier diet because you grow or raise much of it yourself.

8. **Less stress** – not having to worry so much about earning money to pay never-ending utility bills results in less stress. And because you are happier and more active, your sleep patterns are better, and that also lowers stress.

9. **Going back to your roots** – off-grid living used to be the norm; it's only fairly recently that people have come to rely so heavily on the infrastructure provided for them. Get rid of your dependence on that infrastructure, and you go back to living the way you always did – and it's worth bearing in mind that there were less stress and less illness in those days.

10. **Knowledge preservation** – by going off-grid and living a sustainable life, people preserve knowledge for many generations to come. Living in a high-consumer world means this knowledge disappears, and, eventually, it will disappear forever.

11. **Using fewer resources** – it's simple; when you live off-grid, you create more resources than you use, and you use less of the public resources, benefitting everyone.

12. **No more waste and consumerism** – resource consumption is out of control, along with waste. To reduce it, you need to start creating resources instead of just using them. With a renewable, sustainable lifestyle, you help everyone.

13. **Healthier lifestyle** – plenty of fresh air and healthier food are two great benefits: you spend more time outside, and you grow your own food without using pesticides and chemicals.

14. **Building stuff** – this applies to everyone, but preppers in particular – you get to build and make things that you wouldn't normally think about: buildings to live in, storage places, electricity plants (on a small scale, obviously), water gathering and storage, and so on.

15. **You are independent** – because you no longer have to rely on public services and the system, you become more self-reliant and independent, living in a way that suits you.

# Common Misconceptions about Off-Grid Living

For preppers the world over, living off-grid is the ultimate solution for when the SHTF. It makes perfect sense to be independent, to not be in a mess should all services and systems fail in a disaster scenario. However, few preppers really attempt to do it properly, and some try and give up fairly quickly. Much of that is down to some of the most common misconceptions and the fact that people realize it takes a great deal of preparation, and money, to live off-grid successfully. A lack of preparation, coupled with a lack of staying power, means many are doomed to fail - needlessly because it only takes planning and preparation to be successful. Some of the more common misconceptions about off-grid living include:

### 1. I Only Need a Harbor Freight Solar Kit

Many people think this is all they need to power their house, but can you survive on just 45 watts of power? A laptop takes 30 watts to charge up, and your phone will take five watts, but if you're thinking of running lighting, heating, cooking, and other systems, then one of these won't make the cut.

### 2. It Will Be Easy to Wash My Clothes

There are so many gadgets for off-grid clothes washing, but none of them are going to make your life any easier. Having help to wash your clothes is always desirable, but it isn't difficult to do a hand wash. All you need is a large sink or tub, and a way of drying them. And that is where true off-gridders differ from those who are just playing – they are more concerned about how to get their clothes dry.

If you have great weather, you can dry your clothes outside, but what if it's pouring with rain? If there's a blizzard? Below freezing? Then it becomes a problem. If you have a big, fancy house, with a big fancy solar heating and electric system, then it won't be an issue, but most off-gridders go more simplistic than that. You will need to invest in drying racks and be prepared for things to take a couple of days to dry off. Alternatively, if you have the room, set aside a room or a small shed outside, set it up with a washing line and wood-burning stove, and dry your clothes that way. Alternatively, if things really are desperate, you can always pay someone to do it for you!

### 3. Solar Panels on the Roof Are a Great Idea!

While many people think this way, the roof is actually the worst place to put your solar panels. Roofs are hot – heat rises – and that kind of heat actually decreases how efficient your solar panels are. Plus, if you need to maintain them, brush off some snow, or clean them, the roof is high up and awkward to get to.

Stick to ground-mounting your solar panels – you can have more than you can on your roof and benefit from more free power and a better way of maintaining them.

### 4. You Don't Have any Backups – For Anything

When you generate your own power, you don't have a power company to help when something goes wrong. Sometimes, that's not a bad thing; however, you still need a power source, and that means having a backup – for everything. You should have a backup plan for every source of power you need – cooking, heating, showers, food storage, lights, and so on.

### 5. Thinking You Don't Need Propane

Propane is an off-grid necessity, especially for those who don't have thousands of dollars to spend on a state-of-the-art solar system. Most standard solar systems are nowhere near enough to power everything you need. You could probably get away with not using it if your heating was wood and you had a heat changer fitted to it, but in the dead of winter, do you really want to wait a couple of hours for the heating to kick in and the water to heat? Probably not - you need propane.

### 6. Thinking That a Wood Stove is "Living the Dream"

Many off-gridders use wood stoves but think of the work - chopping wood every day to make sure you have enough. And you've got to be somewhere where there is enough wood to chop and live off. Then you have to clean out the stove, build it up - every day. Chop, stack, move wood, cleaning the fire building it - every single day. That's what no one tells you; how hard it is. Your day would be something like this:

*Wake up in a cold house every winter morning. Fly out of bed to get the fire going again and stack some logs on it. Oh, but you forgot to bring any in last night, so out you go, in the freeing air to get some. By the time you get home from work, the fire has died down - another cold house. Off you go again, bringing in more wood, building a fire up. By the time you've dealt with the snakes that just love to hibernate in woodpiles and cleaned up the mess you made bringing the wood in, you're done for the day, and you haven't even thought about dinner, a shower, and settling down in front of the television.*

Does that sound like living the dream? Or would you rather press a button on your solar or propane system and have a warm house in minutes?

## 7. Thinking that Solar Tracking is Vital

Many solar newbies make this mistake, fitting pole-mounted systems to let their solar panels track the sun. Want to know a secret? Forget that; add another solar panel to your existing system instead. You'll save a ton of money and generate far more power. A solar tracker may improve your gain by around 20 percent – for a 1 kW system, you might now get 1.2 kW. However, they cost a fortune, at least a thousand bucks, and you need huge footings made of concrete – it will cost you around $1,500 in total. Buy an extra panel at around $250, and you can bump your system up to 1.5kw in one day. For less money, you get more power, and there are no moving parts that can potentially break.

## 8. Thinking That Propane Fridge and DC Appliance are Worth Buying

Yes, DC is way more efficient, and it does use power to invert DC to AC, but there are other things to consider. Many myths come from once true, now false, information, and the biggest problem is relying on what you see on the internet. There are plenty of old, out-of-date websites, and lots of people take what they read as gospel.

These days, inverter technology has come a long way, and panels cost less. It is not efficient to invert DC to AC, but by adding an extra solar panel or two, what you lose is more than made up for. Weigh that up against what special DC appliances cost and the math is pretty simple.

You also have to consider that many electricians don't like working on DC systems, and a lot won't touch them. Plus, the DC appliance market is small, which tends to mean higher prices. The best option is to go for an AC power system and add more solar panels.

# The Realities of Living Off-Grid

For many people, the thought of living off-grid brings to mind visions of apocalypse survivors, MRE food rations, and piles of ammo – not to mention long-haired hermits grubbing around for food.

You do need to consider an off-grid lifestyle when you draw up your prepping plans, but the reality is often far from what you see in the movies. Do it right, and you can have lighting at the flick of a button, toilets that flush, a fridge that cools your food, and warm water for a shower.

Think about the long and distant past – your ancestors lived off-grid! Even emperors and kings had to rely on fire for heat and light and used water directly from wells and rivers. They didn't have the luxury of water and power at their fingertips, and you might not either, not in the event of a serious SHTF scenario.

Some choose to reduce their dependence on the grid, to do their bit to save the environment, and some want to live a self-sufficient life. For the prepper, self-sufficiency is key, but you do need to know what challenges you face as well as the rewards you reap.

### The Challenges and Rewards

Right now, you might spend time posting pics of your latest holiday on Instagram, spend the evenings watching your favorite Netflix shows or grab a cheeky latte on your way to work. You may still be able to do all those things, but you'll also have to factor in chopping and stacking firewood, tending to your livestock, growing your garden and foraging for food, not to mention building your home. While there are plenty of challenges, there are also many rewards too.

### 1. Food Is a Massive Responsibility

It should be your top priority, together with water. You must have a reliable source of safe food, and establishing a pesticide-free source of produce and livestock free of antibiotics and raised humanely is a challenge in itself. You have to set it all up, maintain your garden and your animals, and you have to be prepared to butcher your own meat. And when you've done that, and brought your harvest in, you have to store it in a way that it will last, and not spoil or go to waste.

The other side of the hard work is the reward – a safe source of tasty food. Prepping for survival isn't all about eating tinned and packet food; it's about storing your own meat, eggs, poultry, and produce so that you can have decent healthy meals to eat, all cooked on a wood or solar stove. It doesn't get any better than that.

### 2. You May Have to Build a House

The modern housing people live in now is not designed for off-grid living. Leave the power off for one week, and you will soon see mold and damp, and you'll probably be growing your own penicillin in the fridge. Many off-gridders, particularly preppers, build a separate house designed to be off-grid. And the reason you see so many off-grid houses out in the middle of nowhere is that building codes in the city ae expensive and restrictive.

This is probably the largest DIY project you will ever undertake but look at in terms of the freedom you will have. You can build your home out of any material you choose, even down to using renewable resources, and you design it around off-grid living. You build your house exactly how you want it.

### 3. What You Don't Do Isn't Getting Done

When you live off-grid, you don't have the luxury of being passive or procrastinating about things. If you don't do it, it won't get done. You may have to spend the spring and summer months gathering, chopping, splitting, and stacking wood. You'll need to be on top of your garden and your livestock, to bring in as much bounty as you can while caring for them.

Nobody is going to empty your composting toilet, your clothes won't hang themselves on the line, and your line won't buzz to tell you that your clothes are dry, either. And that tasty, creamy cheese and butter? If you don't go milk the cow or the goat, you won't get it; it's as simple as that.

Money may be a concern, and some people continue to work while living off-grid. You don't have to if you live in the right community. You can grow more produce and sell it at the markets, barter with your neighbors, learn to knit and sew to make goods for selling, and so on. Everyone has a skill that they can make some money from, but what you won't have to do is clock-watch - punch in on time, attend a staff meeting and all the other irritating parts of on-grid living. Once you become self-sufficient, living a sustainable, renewable life, your financial needs will be small.

### 4. Weathering the Storm

Everyone knows what it's like for the power to go out for whatever reason. When you live with all the comforts that you get with a public service grid, you really are at its mercy. You have to wait for the water to come back on, or the power to be reconnected - there is nothing you can do.

Go off-grid, and it's all in your hands. It may be hard work, but you will have the luxury of power, water, heating, and everything else you need for when a major storm hits. When the storm warning is given, the city folk head to the stores and panic-buy; you can light your fire, and sit there with a warm cup of cocoa and watch it roll in, warm, safe, and secure.

### 5. Not Everyone Will Understand

Your off-grid life will be very different from the way many people live, and while some will be curious about your choice, others will be downright derisive. Your conversation may revolve around a rotational crop and livestock plan while others are discussing the latest *Riverdale* episode – you may never have seen it. You may, for a while, feel that you are cut off from reality until you remember that your reality is fresh fruit waiting to be picked, fresh eggs every day, a warm house in the evening that doesn't rely on the power grid supplying you.

Normal life is what you make of it and, challenging though it will be, it will also be the most rewarding way of life – you will seriously wonder why you didn't do it before.

# Homesteading 101

The definition of 'Homesteading' is "any dwelling with land and buildings where you make a home." Sounds simple, right? Today, homesteading is used as a term for those who try to be self-sufficient, although it is still your home.

## Different Types of Homesteading

Homesteading isn't just a plot of land with a building on it; there are four different primary types of homesteading:

### *Apartment Homesteading*

Think of a traditional homestead and then pare it down to apartment size. Homesteading is all about self-sufficiency, and you can do that in an apartment:

- **Container Gardening** – if you have a balcony, pop some containers out there and plant some vegetables and fruits. If your balcony is big enough, you could even have a small greenhouse.
- **Small Livestock** – got a big enough balcony? Ask your landlord for permission and keep a couple of hens or rabbits – fresh eggs and meat every year.

- **Preserve Food** – you don't need a ton of space to do this, just a freezer and some canning knowledge. Even if you don't grow your own food, you can buy it when it's on sale and store it for yourself.
- **Grow Herbs** – you can do this is in the kitchen or on the balcony and have fresh herbs all year round.
- **Make Pantry Staples** – buy things like flour and sugar in bulk and make cookie mixes, pancake mixes, and so on. You can make your own stuffing, sauces, butter, cream, etc., with just a little bit of knowledge and getting the ingredients at the right price.

## *Small and Large Scale Homesteading*

These are the typical homesteads, usually found in rural areas and with land to grow crops and raise livestock. Even in a small garden, you can have a greenhouse, grow vegetables, have fruit trees, raise some livestock, and more. With a larger garden, you can do it all on a much larger scale.

On a small homestead, you may not be able to grow enough food for livestock for winter months, so you may have to purchase hay from a local farmer. A larger homestead will give you the land you need to do this yourself, and you can keep larger livestock too, including cattle as well as goats.

## *Urban Homesteading*

Urban homesteaders have smaller gardens, usually in subdivisions, where they grow some produce, keep smaller livestock, like hens and ducks, and if they can get permission, rabbits, and goats too. All it takes is permission to do it, a creative mind, and the get-up-and-go to make it work.

# Basic Homestead Steps

To start a small homestead today, there are some important things to keep in mind:

1. **Plan ahead** – don't just get up one morning and decide to do it. You need a plan and short-term and long-term goals. Are you going to be entirely or partly self-sufficient for food? Are you going off-grid? And more. Try and do it without a plan, and you will run into trouble.

2. **Energy Sources** – if you plan to go off-grid, pick a renewable energy source like solar, hydropower, wood, wind, and so on.

3. **Learn to Winterize** – your home must be livable and comfortable in the winter, so learn how to winterize: cleaning gutters, cleaning woodstoves and pipes, cutting and stocking wood, caging your trees and plants to keep them safe, what to do with your livestock, and so on.

4. **Start Gardening** – if you are going to be self-sufficient, you need to know how to garden. You can, if you do it right, keep your produce supply going all year round. And if you grow too much, you can always sell or trade it. Learn what vegetables and fruits ripen when so you can have a year-round garden, grow herbs for cooking and medicine, and learn about crop rotation and companion planting to get the best out of your garden.

5. **Have the Right Pet** – many homesteaders have a large dog, not just as a companion but for protection for you and your livestock. You can also consider cats to keep rodents and snakes down and minimize the damage done to your garden.

6. **Choose your Livestock Wisely** – chickens are dead simple to keep, and you get eggs and meat from them. Rabbits are a good choice too; bred right, you get a good source of meat and fur. Geese and ducks make great homesteading pets,

and if you have the time and space, a cow or two, goats, sheep, even a pig. All of these create food and other byproducts that will help you in your sustainable lifestyle.

7. **Don't Neglect Tools and Weapons** - a knife is a must as it can be used for multiple jobs. Be aware that you will also need to do work around your homestead, so you will need a variety of tools: screwdrivers, saws, hammers, nails, screws, and so on. And don't forget weapons - a gun for hunting and security is a must, along with plenty of ammunition.

8. **Make Your Own** - learn how to make basic items such as clothes, soap, candles, and so on. That way, you are not reliant on anyone else for your household goods.

9. **Never Waste Anything** - people tend to waste food and water because it's easy to restock, but when you become self-sufficient, you can't do that. Every egg, scrap of meat, vegetable, fur, and so on must be used. Gather all the water you can, use every inch of your garden, and never let anything that can be used for something go to waste.

These are the basics. To be fair, one of the easiest ways to start being self-sufficient is to start with a small garden. You don't have to grow everything from scratch - get cuttings from others and grow things that reseed and shoot up extras every year, multiplying your crops easily. Here are some examples:

- **Raspberries** - these fruit bushes send new shoots up yearly. With just one plant, you could soon have a whole row, although you will need to cull the older ones within a few years.

- **Strawberries** - these send out runners which root themselves, growing new plants. Do be aware, though, that the more runners your plants send out, the less likely you are to have much fruit, so do cut some out, or repot them and sell/swap them.

- **Willow trees** – if these grow in your area, simply snip off a baby branch, put in water, and wait for the roots to sprout. It won't take long to get a few trees going like that.
- **Quaking aspens** – these are constantly dropping babies and multiplying all over the place.
- **Potatoes** – if you bought a sack of spuds and didn't eat them all, leave them to grow shoots and then pop them in some dirt. You can even grow these in tubs indoors, so long as they get natural light and don't freeze.
- **Herbs** – most herbs are simple to grow and require nothing more than digging a bit of the plant up and popping it in another patch of dirt.

# Solar Energy and Other Power Options

Going off-grid means choosing the right off-grid power sources. Most people wouldn't have the first clue where to start, and many only really consider using solar power. You don't have to leave your city or hometown to go off-grid, or partially off-grid; with the latest leaps and bounds made in technology, there are plenty of renewable options you can fit to any property.

The following are five realistic renewable sources for off-grid power – the first being the most obvious:

**Solar Power**

Using solar electricity, you can plug in and power your home quite easily. Most opt for a sun-powered system consisting of photovoltaic panels, batteries, and an inverter. Set up right, these can provide a lot of power, especially if you live in a sunny area. There are no moving parts, and they last for quite a while without needing repair. The downside is the cost. Very rarely is it cost-effective to run your entire home off solar power, and you do have to bear in mind solar exposure – some areas don't get as much as others, and for most people, solar is part of the system, not the whole system.

Most people don't put solar panels on their roof for two reasons – it isn't cheap, and it doesn't look nice. There is also the fact that they need cleaning now and then, and going up on your roof isn't the safest. Some people opt for *solar roof tiles*; they are smaller, look like standard tiles, and are tough. If you are building a new off-grid home, consider putting these on all or part of your roof, especially if it is a single-story home. Do keep in mind that they are not cheap, and an area of 2,500 square feet would cost between $20,000 and $50,000 – you may be able to get tax incentives in some areas.

If you look at it over the long-term, going full solar can see your electricity bill come down to zero or, if you go partial-solar, you can cut the bill by 40-60%, And the tiles do last for 30+ years so, given time, it will pay for itself.

**Residential Wind Turbine**

The wind is definitely a renewable source, not to mention sustainable, and using a residential wind turbine, you can tap into it for your off-grid power system. These are much smaller now than they used to be and can easily be installed in a residential area.

If you have an acre or more of land and you live in a windy area, it is a great option to consider. A typical system, producing 10kW, will cost from $50,000 to $60,000. It is expensive, but you can save 90-100 percent of your monthly bill, and it pays for itself in six years. Some countries/states even offer tax incentives of up to 30 percent, so be sure to check out what's on offer in your region. Do be aware, though, that if you don't get much breeze in your area, the wind turbine will not move, and that means no electricity. Plus, there are moving parts that wear out and need maintenance, not to mention which also have the potential to fail.

**Geothermal Heat Pump**

Geothermal energy is one of the cleanest and most sustainable forms of heat energy coming from under the earth's surface and supplying energy all day, every day. Geothermal plants are used for harnessing the energy for industrial use, but now you can use a geothermal heat pump to do the same at home. A geothermal pump is both a heating and cooling system, using the ground to source energy in the cold winters and the using the earth in the summer as a heat sink. You can build it as a separate system or have it integrated with your HVAC; it's your choice,

Geothermal pumps work like a refrigerator – they transfer heat from the earth around your house, using pipes filled with water or antifreeze. These pipes attach to the pump, which becomes a heater or a cooling system, depending on the external temperatures.

### Micro-Hydro Electricity

If your property has a running water source, such as a stream or brook, you can consider using a micro-hydro system to produce power. Hydro systems use water, using water flowing from a high to a low place, to generate power, and the micro-hydro systems convert running water flows into rotational energy. That is turned into electricity using a waterwheel, pump, or turbine.

These systems are much easier to build and a good deal cheaper than wind or solar power, but the primary downside is that it can only work in specific conditions. If you don't have that running water source, you can't use the system. If you are lucky enough to be able to use it, you can generate up to 100 times the power that a solar or wind-powered system does for the same start-up capital, giving you an unlimited source of energy. It is more consistent, and fewer batteries are needed for storage because the source is harvesting energy all the time.

### Hybrid Solar/Wind System

To go completely off-grid, you could use a system that makes the best of fluctuating weather systems. That is a hybrid system and is far more reliable because you do not depend on a single source for your energy. It also works out cheaper because each source's components are smaller than if you used just one system.

As a rough guide, you could have a hybrid system that generates 7-8kWh per day for around $35,000, double the wattage, and the cost goes up to about $60,000.

With technology in wind, solar, water, and geothermal energy advancing all the time, it is now much easier to install an off-grid system just about anywhere. Systems are smaller, and while the initial layout is expensive, you can expect prices to come down as time passes.

# Water Sources, Solutions, and Systems

While generating power is an important part of the off-grid or homestead lifestyle, water systems should be an equal priority. People take water for granted; the average person will not give a thought to using up to 100 gallons per day, much of that wasted. Start living a sustainable lifestyle, and everything you learned will go out of the window.

Having a good, reliable, and safe water source is not a backup plan; it is primary and necessary. Most people don't know where to start, though, and what they need to consider. While it is great if you have a pond or a stream on your property, you shouldn't rely on it. The best way is to set up a diverse system to ensure that you are never left without this precious lifeblood.

This guide won't tell you how to build a system; it will give you an idea of what you can use and the pros and cons of each one.

## Off-Grid Water Sources

There are three primary forms of off-grid water: below ground, above ground, and precipitation. If you can, you want access to all of these sources as it will give you the best chance of ensuring you never run out.

### Well Water

A well can bring up water from deep in the ground, up to 300 feet or deeper. If you already have a well, fantastic, you're off to a good start. If not, consider having one. Instead of using an electric pump to draw the water, convert it to wind or solar power.

*Pros*

- A reliable freshwater source
- Sink it deep enough, and it won't freeze in the winter
- Relatively clean, although you should filter it before you drink it

*Cons*

- It takes energy to get the water, be it manual pumping or another method of powering a pump.
- It's a gamble – you may not hit water in your area
- It is expensive, several thousand dollars
- Your water may have been polluted, especially if you are in a fracking area

### Rain Collection

Rain is free water, and you should collect as much of it as you can. Make sure you have enough water storage tubs to collect and store the rain to get you through dry periods. Generally, rainwater is clean, soft, and has none of the chemicals in public service water and the excessive minerals found in underground water.

*Pros*

- The system is easy to implement
- It's clean and free water, so long as you have an impervious surface for it to land on. Be aware that asphalt roofing can leach chemicals into the water

*Cons*

- Some areas have restrictions in rainwater collection
- You must have an impervious surface to collect the water, and you will need water storage facilities beside the collection area

**Ponds**

Ponds are for more than ducks to swim in; they're also a backup source of water. You shouldn't use one as a primary drinking source, but it's a great resource that can potentially save your life and benefit anything that lives on your land.

*Pros*

- If you already have one, they are easy to maintain
- It fills when it rains and provides a fabulous habitat for plants and animals

*Cons*

- Pond water must be thoroughly cleaned before consumption
- A pump is needed to transport the water out of the pond and into storage
- Getting it from the pond to your house is not easy

**Springs**

Springs are a wonderful source of clean cold water, and if you have one on your property, you are richer than many homesteaders and off-gridders.

*Pros*

- The water is sparkling clean, free, and once you have an infrastructure built around it, requires little care

*Cons*

- Building the initial infrastructure to harness the water needs work and it may not be in a convenient area

- They can be contaminated by your neighbors, deliberately or accidentally

## Off-grid Water Utilization Systems

It is one thing having a source of water, quite another to store and use it. There are several storage systems you can consider:

### Rain Barrels

You can buy these or make them from food storage barrels.

*Pros*

- Install them wherever you have a downspout - when it rains, instant water storage
- Small enough that they can be used on most types of property
- Raised on a platform, you can get a decent amount of pressure from them

*Cons*

- If you buy them, you are limited to 55 gallons, and you'll need many of them. You can make a chain of them, joining them with overflow pipes. When it rains, and the first barrel fills, it overflows to the second, and so on - the more you have, the more water you collect

### Cisterns

Cisterns have been used for millions of years, and you can locate them above the ground or below it. They can be made out of just about any material, even stone, metal, or Ferrocement. Locate them at a higher elevation than the tap, and you have a passive pressure system.

*Pros*

- You can store thousands of gallons of water

- Bury it in the ground, and it won't freeze

*Cons*

- Constructing them is intensive
- You need to have a decent understanding of your terrain
- You need a lot of space, and if you want pressure, you need elevation

### Lugging Buckets

A high proportion of the world's population still uses buckets to carry water, and you can do it too.

*Pros*

- There's nothing to break down – just have a spare bucket

*Cons*

- You need to be reasonably fit
- Your buckets must be spotless
- You should use food-grade buckets

## Determining When Water Doesn't Need Filtering

You might think that this is silly and that all water needs to be filtered and purified before you can drink it – but it doesn't. Doing it when you don't need to is just a waste of time, not to mention also a waste of precious resources. This is another reason why you should have a diverse system because it lets you make the right choices for your requirements at any given time. All you need to determine, as far as water goes, is what is for human consumption – the rest doesn't matter.

Take watering your garden or your livestock, for example – raw water is just fine for them. Trees are one of the best water filters there are, and you can purchase a filtering system that makes use of them to clean the water. Alternatively, just use rain barrels – plain old ran water is perfectly okay for plants and animals.

Unfiltered rainwater or well water can also be used for doing your washing – there is little point in cleaning and filtering the water only to chuck dirty clothes and washing detergent in it. Hanging your clothes on the line in sunlight disinfects them – sunlight is nature's disinfectant – and you may not have time to get the washing in before an unexpected storm hits, giving your clothes an extra wash in rainwater.

For cooking, cleaning, and drinking, the water must be filtered.

# The Off-Grid Budget: How Much Will It Cost?

Money really does make the world go 'round, and you are going to need a fair stash to get started on your off-grid lifestyle. First, you need to clear any debt you have, then you need capital, and the answer to how much it costs is different for everyone because it depends on how much you do and how far you are prepared to go.

So, these estimates may not all apply to you; focus on those that do and keep in mind that they are only a rough guide.

**Property – $0 to $25,000 (average)**

You may be lucky enough to find a plot of land going cheap or even free, but keep one thing in mind – there is a reason why. The plot may not be right, and often, free land comes with conditions attached (often not free).

If you are prepared to spend money to get exactly what you want, then expect to pay upwards of $20,000+ for up to five acres. You may get a better deal, so shop around and do your homework first. If you intend to be completely self-sufficient, including growing food, the states that have the best potential are:

- Arkansas
- California

- Florida
- Hawaiian Islands
- Kentucky
- Missouri
- New jersey
- North Carolina
- Texas

**Shelter – $0 to $150,000 (average)**

Do your homework, and you may even be able to purchase land with a house already on it. If not, you need to factor in road access and the costs of building a home on the land. If you are clever and handy, timber from your own land could be used or get in touch with the local forestry commission – sometimes, a company will pay you to let them clear your land.

Failing that, a contractor will be needed; the average cost of a stick frame house in the USA is between $120,000 and $150,000. If you want to pay more, a rammed earth house will set you back around $200,000, and if your budget is much lower, consider purchasing a manufactured, single-wide dwelling for about $20,000.

Keep in mind that you do not want to get into any debt over this, so start small and increase over time.

**Wind/Solar Power – $1,000 to $37,000 (average)**

Providing power requires a minimum of one solar panel or a wind turbine and an inverter. This costs around $1,000, but you will only get enough power for a small chest freezer or a solar fridge. Add more solar panels and turbines – try for a combination to ensure you always get power. To power an entire home, you would need a system costing around $30,000.

If you do not want to depend on the grid, you will need storage batters and these cost up to $300 each. A full back-up system will cost around $7,000, and don't forget that your batteries will need replacing every three years or so. Check with local server farms - you may be able to get used batteries a bit cheaper.

### A Well - $5,000 to $20,000 (average)

If you are lucky, your land may already have a freshwater source on it, but if you use lake or stream water, you will need to clean and filter it first. If there is no fresh water, you'll need a well, and that involves drilling a large hole and using a pump to get the water out. You may not have to go too far down to find water, in which case it will be much cheaper than having to go deeper.

The average depth is 50-100 feet; expect to pay up to $100 per foot. Then you need a good pump, costing around $800-$2,000, all the plumbing and the electrical work, and water storage tanks, which cost $500-$1,000 each.

If you want more than one well, you could consider purchasing a hydraulic drilling rig, costing $10,000-$15,000, but if you live in a preppers community or an off-grid area, you can always make a little money back by digging wells for others.

### Septic System - $2,500 to $5,000 (average)

Properly maintained, a septic system can last for up to 40 years, and they are not too expensive to construct. The biggest cost consideration is your soil - if it doesn't drain well, your tank will be more expensive. Make sure you talk to any contractor bidding for the job about this.

### Composting Toilet - $100 to $5,000 (average)

Composting toilets are a must as they break solid human waste into fertilizer in the same way that kitchen scraps are broken down. They use heat, oxygen, aerobic bacteria, and time, eventually producing "humanure". The good thing is that little to no water is required, but they do require upkeep and maintenance.

Purchase a self-contained unit for up to $2,000 or build your own for as little as $100 per bathroom. Alternatively, spend around $10,000 or more for a centralized system that connects several toilets and one composter.

**Greywater System – $500 to $10,000 (average)**

Greywater systems are used to collect shower, sink, washing machine, and dishwasher water so you can use it in your garden or to flush toilets. These vary depending on the complexity of the system and whether it is being installed when you build your home or added afterward.

A simple system could be as little as $500, while a more complex system, collecting all greywater, a filtration system, and storage could cost $10,000 or more.

**Geothermal Heat Pump – $7,500 to $20,000 (average)**

These take heat from about eight feet below the ground and use it for heating in the winter and cooling in the summer. Again, the cost will be based on how large your home is, your insulation, how much space you have to install a heat exchanger loop field, and whether you are adding it after building your home or during the construction.

**Gardening – $100 to $2,500 (average)**

For a family of four, you will need around 1,000 sq. feet of land per person to produce enough fruit and vegetables. Seeds will cost you around $100 per year, but once you get started, you can harvest seeds from some plants.

You will also require a fence, which will set you back up to $1,000 for a woven wire fence supported with chicken wire – chain link costs more. You could also use wood from your land to construct your own fence. You will also require some kind of irrigation system – keep your gray water system in mind when you do this.

If you want to grow nut and fruit trees, grapes, and berries, you will need a variety, and this can cost $15-$100+ per bush or tree. Don't forget to start a compost bin or pile somewhere to help feed your new plants.

**Livestock - $1,000 to $4,000 (average) + average monthly cost $300+**

Chickens are one of the cheapest to keep, and you can usually pick them up for no more than $10 each. You want to average one laying hen for every person. Then you need a chicken coop - if you have scrap lumber, use that, but do make sure it is secure, or you can buy one for $150+.

A breeding pig will cost up to $3,000, and pigs for meat cost up to $100. Two pigs will feed four people for a year. You also need a pigpen with strong fencing and shelter, which could cost upwards of $500. Expect to spend around $50 per month on food, but you can cut that by adding table and garden scraps to their menu.

A cow will set you back between $1,000 and $3,000, depending on the breed. One cow is enough to feed four people for a year, and cattle food is around $200 per month - again, supplement with garden scraps or have a pasture. You need an acre of land per cow, and fencing will cost upwards of $2,500, depending on the pasture size.

If you purchase a milking cow, you can save on milk, cream, cheese, butter, ice cream, etc., and you can opt to breed, raising calves for money or meat.

**Outbuildings - $2,000 to $30,000 (average)**

A greenhouse cost will differ depending on size. If you just want a small one for starting seeds early, you could buy a kit for around $750, but if you want to go large and grow vegetables all year round, expect to pay around $10,000. Alternatively, build your own out of materials you can salvage cheap or free.

A barn will depend on the features you want - feed storage, tack room, stalls, height, flooring, electricity, water, and so on. You can build a small one for anywhere between $10-$15 per sq. foot or you can go for a steel frame construction, costing $8-$10 per sq. foot. Expect to spend between $10,000-$20,000 (average).

A chicken coop may be built for free from scrap material, or you can buy one from as little as $150 for a basic four-hen coop. If you want something more special, expect to pay up to $1,500.

If you don't have a barn and you want to keep cats, you can build cat houses out of ice chests for $100 or less, or you can purchase a wooden one for $350+.

Lastly, a root cellar is a great way of storing food. A small barrel system costs less than $100, or you can build whatever size you want - the bigger you go, the more expensive it is.

## Maintenance Costs

Once you've spent the money to construct your off-grid home, you still need money to maintain it. Aim to spend around $1,000 a month, although if you are a serious prepper, you've already got most of these bases covered:

- **Food** - even growing your own produce and raising livestock will still leave you needing certain items: rice, pasta, baking ingredients, etc.
- **Household** - light bulbs, heating oil, tools, cleaning products, toilet paper, and so on
- **Gasoline** - your equipment and vehicles will need oil and fuel
- **Taxes** - unless you are in an apocalypse situation and the entire system is down, you still need to pay taxes
- **Insurance** - car insurance, health insurance, even property insurance will be needed

- **Health care** – this is a huge consideration: whether you have health insurance or you put money aside for emergencies, it's still going to cost you

In the final part of this preppers guide, you are going to look at SHTF Survival.

# PART THREE: SHTF SURVIVAL

# 10 SHTF Scenarios: What to Expect and What to Do

Many people believe that preppers are only focused on apocalyptic scenarios and do nothing more than hoard food, water, weapons, and survival gadgets. This is a stereotype that only a small percentage of preppers fall into, and it isn't a bad thing. Prepping, to that extent, can be fun to do and keeps you occupied.

However, prepping should really be about all types of SHTF scenarios, not just TEOTWAWKI scenarios – The End Of The World As We Know It –, and stereotyping just makes it all the more difficult to convince others to start prepping.

Prepping is about preparation to survive, and that doesn't just involve apocalyptic scenarios where death is almost a certainty. It means being prepared for anything, including these top ten scenarios, from financial hardship right up to the apocalypse. Before you begin prepping in earnest for the biggest, make sure you have covered every base, including prepping for realistic, more likely to happen scenarios first; then you can build on that for the bigger ones:

### One – Financial Hardship

You may think you have a stable job, you may think your finances are safe, but anything can happen, and that includes a temporary or longer-term shut-down of the banking system.

Unexpected hardship is dangerous, and it can come in multiple forms – job loss, divorce, illness or serious injury, several large unexpected bills for repairs. Anything can throw a spanner in the works. Here is what you need to do to prep for a scenario like this, and if it never happens, then you have a financial fallback for when a bigger SHTF scenario occurs:

- Pay off your debts and have enough money to cover at least six months' salary. You'll need to do this gradually – pay a bit extra off your debts and put a certain amount aside each week or month to save up.
- Make sure you have medical/health insurance that's up to date, not to mention car, house, and any other important insurance.
- Start stocking food and basic supplies. Aim for a minimum of three months' water and food supplies for the whole family and make sure you do the same for household supplies – toilet paper, toiletries, cleaning products, and so on.
- Make friends. A good community is the best way to survive – be it a church, neighbors, and so on. Build strong relationships that can stand the test of time. Help others when they need it, and they will return the favor.

**Two – Natural Disasters (Small-Scale)**

Think about your particular area – are there any natural phenomena that regularly occur, such as earthquakes, floods, hurricanes, tornadoes, snowstorms, and so on? These are the first SHTF scenarios to plan for – most people watch the news, and they see how these natural disasters are getting worse by the year. To prep for these:

- Do your research. Find out what occurs in and near your area. Run Google searches, get in touch with your nearest weather resource, ask people in the area – if something has happened in the past, it can surely happen again.

- Do more research. Contact FEMA and other US agencies to get ideas on how to prep and what the emergency evacuation plans are for your area.
- Prepare your supplies. Aim for a three-month minimum supply of essentials – if you did your financial hardship prepping, you already have this. Then, depending on how bad things get in your area, double it. Start early; at the first hint of a disaster, your local stores will run out of stock very quickly. And invest in waterproof containers to store everything high off the ground.
- Make sure your building is easy to evacuate and have a family plan in place. In the event of a bad SHTF scenario, evacuation is the likely course of action. Make sure you have gas in your vehicle, spare gas, bug-out bags with the essentials, and copies of important documents in every bug-out bag. Got pets? Even they need their own bug-out bag, so don't forget to factor them into your plans.

**When the SHTF**

- Make sure you have a way of following the news, so you are up to date on the latest events. And DO follow the official advice given in your area – if you are told to evacuate, do it. And don't waste time; the last thing you want is to be trapped. If you do need to be rescued, make sure you help the emergency teams, not hinder them.

This might all seem like obvious advice, but take this story of a prepper:

He wasn't a newbie; he had been doing it for years and knew exactly what to do. When the SHTF and his town was flooded, he hung back, thinking he could be a hero and save people. He ended up getting in the way of the emergency services, stopped a whole load of people from leaving because he told them he had more than enough supplies, and they all wound up perched on his roof. They needed to be airlifted; luckily, they were all saved, but it could have been so much worse. Do not be that person. Use common sense and don't be a hero.

### Three – The Grid Goes Down

This covers a broad spectrum, but in essence, this refers to a major disruption, in one way or another, to normal supply. The most common one is the electricity supply, and it could be out for days, depending on what brought it down. It could even be a shortage of fuel.

In small-scale terms, this is common in many areas; when storms hit, the power invariably goes out, and if you live somewhere like Alaska, even Canada, snowstorms can take power down for weeks on end. Here is how to prep:

- Have backups for everything – spare fuel and gas, a generator, and a healthy supply of all the essentials. The best-case scenario is to aim to disconnect entirely from the grid and live off renewable energy sources, much like you do with off-grid homesteading. This may not be possible for everyone, so as a minimum, have a generator and fuel.

- Make sure you can communicate. When the grid goes down, and you can't travel far, being able to communicate with others is key. Keep a basic mobile phone on hand, fully charged – the old type that lasts for days on a single charge. If the mobile system fails, make sure you have a radio setup.

### Four – Civil Unrest/Violence/Crime

This is not an uncommon scenario – you only have to look at the news to see just how much civil unrest and rising crime levels there is in the world right now. Could it happen to you? Yes, especially if you live in a highly populated urban area, so here is how to prep for it:

- Make sure you have plenty of food, water, and essentials in stock. During periods of unrest, you don't want to leave your home unless you absolutely have to. Be prepared to hole up and dig in for a while.

- Make sure you have a good neighborhood watch scheme; it's your first and best defense against riots and violence in your area. That doesn't mean not calling the police when trouble starts, but it does mean that you are all watching each other's backs. When things are particularly bad, you could set up a schedule, so your street is being watched at all times. Make sure you have a way of communicating with one another and make plans for what to do if the unrest or violence gets to your street or somebody attempts to enter your home.

- Make sure you have some basic home defense in place, but DO NOT turn vigilante and start firing at anyone who comes near you – that's how innocent lives are lost. Even if you shoot a real criminal, there's a high chance that attention will turn to you in retaliation. If having a gun helps you feel better, then have one, but don't use it unless you absolutely have to. Instead, concentrate on home defense – a tripwire attached to an alarm of some sort often deters small-time looters and criminals. Have a good alarm system and a way to call for assistance if you need it.

- You should also be prepared to barricade yourself inside your home should things get bad. Have shutters over your window, block doors and windows with furniture, and stay away from the windows and doors in case of stray bullets – do leave yourself a means of escape, though – just not a main, obvious entrance.

### Five – Economic Collapse

This isn't quite so likely but has happened and can again. This could mean anything from economic depression to extreme hyperinflation. This would lead to the financial hardship talked about earlier, and it wouldn't be easy to get supplies. In that case, your financial planning prep will see you through.

If things are more extreme, like all financial systems collapsing, any money you have in the bank is useless, trade will be impossible (to start with), and you won't have anything – no money and no supplies – in a world where everyone is panicking.

Unless you prep properly, if the economy collapses, you will be most likely die from violence or a lack of basic essentials, so:

- Stock up on food, and plenty of it.
- Make sure you can produce things, like tools and food, that you can trade. If you can grow food, do it – you're going to need it.
- Be prepared to defend yourself, your family, and your home.

**Six – Cyberattack**

This is becoming more and more likely as each year passes, given the increasing scale of cyberattacks seen now. In a world that is highly connected, the total failure of communications and servers would be a total disaster. What would happen if communication satellites, connected devices, and the internet failed?

Initially, law enforcement, medical care, and trade would break down, accompanied by mass panic. Most governments are prepared for something like this and would likely regain control – eventually. The first weeks or months would be utter chaos, though, and it is down to you to make sure you can survive. Here is how:

- As well as a decent supply of food and other essentials, make sure you have a good stock of information. This refers to copies of your all-important paperwork, certifications, contact information for important contacts (handwritten, not stored on a phone), books that contain useful information you won't have access to online, and so on. You should also keep an up-to-date first aid book and survival books if you can – if not, print it all out from the internet and keep it in waterproof document wallets.

- Have a radio. If all communication satellites collapse, it will be invaluable. Not only is it your way of keeping in contact with others, but it is also the most likely method the government will use to transmit information. Consider amateur ham radio as a hobby; not only is it fun, it could be a lifesaver.

### Seven – Terrorism/War

Once, this wasn't a likely scenario, but now it is. Primarily, this refers to persistent terrorism or large-scale wars that could put the whole nation in a state of war. Not nuclear war, not yet anyway, but bombs and guns being used in urban areas, knocking out travel and communication networks.

While it may not be likely in your area, you should be prepared for it anyway. The only real prep you can do here, aside from keeping your supplies up, is listening to the news – do NOT, however, take all news as being a signal that war is going to break out. Be assured: you will know if it is going to happen.

### Eight – Biological Weapons/Superbugs

This covers anything from an Ebola outbreak to the use of anthrax and other biological weapons. The first is more likely than the latter, not least because of the sheer level of resources needed for a biological weapon capable of killing a whole nation.

On the whole, modern health care and sanitation have people well covered for things like superbugs, but they can still happen, and you should still prep:

- Make sure you have a supply of clean water. Dirty water is often the cause of disease outbreaks and how they are spread. And, face it – if you were going to target a nation, what better way than infecting the water supply? Make sure you have an independent water supply and a top-notch filtration system.

- If you can, have an airtight room that has a great filtration system to ensure you can breathe properly. If not, go old school and have gas masks on hand – do check the rubber seal has not cracked, though.

- Make sure you have excellent sanitation in the event that the sewage system fails. A septic tank will see you through for a while, but you must have a backup in case things go on for longer. If you have a bug-out shelter, ensure it has a good toilet pit, dug away from your water supply (downwards), and away from your shelter. Also, make sure you have a decent supply of cleaning and sanitizer materials and have a quarantine plan in place should any of your group come into contact with a superbug.

### Nine – EMP

An electromagnetic pulse (EMP) is fast becoming a major concern for preppers. An EMP is a huge energy wave that, in theory, could take out every electronic device. People cannot speculate on the likelihood of this happening, and although a solar flare could potentially do it, it isn't likely. However, it is something you should consider, and preparations are the same as for a cyberattack or grid-down scenario.

### Ten – Nuclear Blast

While this was once a big fear, especially during the Cold War, it isn't these days. However, with rising tensions among the world superpowers, the threat is always current. You must also consider the number of major nations that use nuclear energy, and with human error a very real possibility, there is always the potential for another Chernobyl.

You further have to consider nuclear missile attacks – Iran, Korea, Russia, to name a few, are more than capable and ready to launch one at the USA, and that makes it a real threat to be prepared for:

- Make sure you know exactly what to do in the event of a nuclear blast. Your primary priority is shelter and staying away from windows. Obviously, it would be ideal if you had your own nuclear shelter, but most people won't. So the immediate danger is the actual blast – you should have a room prepared with a radio, water, food, blankets, and first aid supplies. It must have no windows, and you should immediately cover your ears and eyes.
- After the initial blast, you will have several minutes to get to a shelter before the fallout begins to hit the ground. Although they don't offer a huge amount of protection, have some potassium iodide pills and take them immediately.
- Stay inside, and have the radio on for official announcements.
- You should have a radiation face mask for each person and a radio in your bug-out or bug-in shelter.
- Make sure you know where you can shelter at work, home, and everywhere along your commute route. And make sure you have a way of communicating with family and friends.
- If you can, build a shelter. You can build something basic in your own home. You don't have to go to the expense of a full-on nuclear fallout shelter.

There is one more scenario to consider, although it is extreme. It is TEOTWAWKI; in other words, the collapse of civilization. This means the government has collapsed, along with law and order, not to mention morality, across a nation.

This is unlikely, and if it does happen, it won't be for long. The human race has resilience, not to mention a mostly stable society. Throughout all the disasters recorded through history, civilization has never totally collapsed, at least not long term.

That said, anything is possible, and you should be prepared for it. Here is how:

- You need to be prepared in every way mentioned for every potential SHTF scenario, but you must think longer term than just a few months.
- Make sure you have enough items to barter with and learn all the skills you possibly can to help you. You won't be able to store enough food for a lifetime, but you can learn how to be self-sufficient.
- Learn a few new languages. Once civilization has collapsed, people are likely to travel across the globe looking for somewhere to live. Even with no trains, planes, or ships, most people will find their way anywhere, just like they did many centuries ago.
- Learn to teach. You may not have kids now, but they're going to be the primary way of ensuring the survival of the human race. Learn how to teach kids everything they need for survival – not just survival skills, but languages, history, literature, pretty much everything they need to make civilization work again.

You cannot possibly prepare for every potential scenario, but you can be prepared for almost anything. Start basic by prepping for disasters in your own area and work from there; eventually, you will be prepared for most things.

# SHTF Evacuation

If you reside in an urban or city area and are interested in prepping for when the SHTF, you will probably already know that getting out of a city is harder in an emergency than it is to escape the suburbs or a smaller town – you only have to look at events in the news to see how true this is.

For example, in 2015, Belgium was locked down for several days. Tanks patrolled the street, and people were forced to stay in their houses. Why? Because of one terrorist running rampage following the November 2015 attacks in Paris.

On New Year's Eve 2015-16, in Cologne, Germany, a mass sexual assault took place, with more than 100 women filing complaints – all on one night and carried out by a group of immigrants (confirmed).

Riots and terrorist attacks are not the only scenarios that might require you to bug out, but whatever the scenario is, you can guarantee one thing – evacuation will not be easy. A combination of checkpoints, traffic jams, and riots will make it hard to get out, and while those who live in smaller towns or rural areas may have made plans to bug in should an SHTF scenario arise, those in the city may not be able to.

What you can do is have an evacuation plan in place to give yourself and your family the very best chance of getting out safely. The plan you draw up must have several aspects that cover the following:

### 1. Assess Your Situation

Before you can even begin to make your plan, you must know your current situation. Everyone has different homes and family lives, and that means different liabilities and assets. Some people rent out their homes. Some live in city high-rises. Some have children, live alone, have pets, or elderly parents living with them. You might have an income of $30,000 per year or $130,000.

You must assess your own situation, so you know what you are working with; planning properly now will save you hassle later on and will ensure your evacuation plan is sound. Some of the things you need to ask yourself are –

- How many people are covered by the plan?
- Are there small children, older people, or those who have a handicap of some kind?
- Are there pets in the household?
- Are you in a remote area, mid-city, downtown?
- Do you have somewhere to go?
- Do you have a means of getting there?
- Do you know when you need to leave?

With those questions answered, now there are four more important ones to answer when you draw up your plan –

### a. Do you NEED to go?

When you draw up your evacuation plan, you should determine if there is a need to go. Many people opt to stay put, bug in, and defend their home, regardless of the situation. Indeed, many serious preppers will tell you that it is best to bug in for many SHTF scenarios, but there are always times when it's necessary to evacuate. It is down to you to work out when you are safe to bug in, or you need to get going, and that means setting criteria to make your decision by.

### b. Do you know WHEN to go?

You may have specific criteria that determine if you need to go or not, such as specific scenarios that require you to bug out. You may opt for bugging out when the grocery stores empty, with no chance of being restocked for some time.

The key point is to make sure those criteria are defined clearly; then, you can determine WHEN to go, should any of those scenarios happen, or are a threat. Leave too early, and you might find you didn't need to leave. Go too late, and you might find it tough to get out of the city; everyone will be trying to get out at the same time, and exit routes will be clogged. You might even find the military has stepped in and shut the roads down.

### c. HOW are you getting out?

Your evacuation plan has to be ready at the drop of a hat, and that means ensuring the following:

- Every member of your evacuation group needs a bug-out bag, even pets.

- Everyone should have everyday items with them all the time – you might be surprised at how many survival tools a keychain or wallet can hold: mini flashlight, multi-tool, mini first-aid kit, weapons for self-defense, whistle, and even something to start a fire with.

- You need hardcopy maps of the entire area. Mark every exit route on them clearly and be aware that main routes are likely to be clogged, so make sure you learn the alternative routes. You must all know at least three routes out of the city to your destination, including power lines and railways, especially if you need to get to your bug-out shelter in a hurry.

- Make sure your bug-out location is near, within 20 to 100 miles of your home. If you are relying on a car, you can be the maximum distance out, but if you need to go on foot, you won't want to be far away. You could also consider using bicycles instead of going on foot - it will be hard work, but you will cover more ground. If you can get to a friend in an unaffected city or town, make sure everyone knows where it is and give them a phone number and address - that person may also be an emergency contact.

- Make sure the vehicle you are using to get away has plenty of gas, no less than half a tank. At the very least, you need enough to get to your emergency location.

- Practice your evacuation plan with everyone involved - several times. When the time comes, you don't want any holdups.

**Additional Tips**

As well as everything discussed, there are a few other things to consider:

- If you can, bug out at night. If the SHTF scenario is a war or a riot, you tend to find that the quietest times are 2 AM to 5 AM. You shouldn't run into any traffic problems, but make sure you know where security checkpoints are so you can avoid them.

- If the situation is urgent enough that you cannot wait, decide immediately whether to use your car or go on foot/bicycle. And be ready to ditch your car at a minute's notice and continue your journey on foot.

- Have supplies and valuables ready to throw in your car when you go.

- Make sure there is a fully loaded bug-out bag in the car - everyone should have their own ready to grab as well.

- Be careful as you leave – depending on the situation, the key is to remain invisible. If you travel at night, try not to use flashlights. If you go by day, do it in a way that won't attract attention.

- You cannot take everyone with you, so don't try, not unless you have infinite supplies and room. It sounds awful, but if you try to be a hero, you could be risking your own life as well as others

- Expect you and your family to become separated at some point. Ensure everyone has a walkie-talkie, a cell phone with extra batteries, a charger, area maps, and knows the set meeting points, as well as the bug-out location and how to get there, regardless of the mode of transport.

### WHERE are you going?

Not everyone will have a comfortable bug-out location with plenty of food and water. If you don't, do not attempt to bug out unless it really is the only option, and it's safer to take a chance in the wilderness than stay at home or stick to the roads. Only you can determine the situations that may require this.

If you have no alternative location to go to, consider a national park or a nearby campground instead.

### Can Anyone Be 100 Percent Ready?

Not really, but that isn't an excuse to slack off on your preparations. Everything you do will help you prep for an SHTF scenario, even if it's just buying a wind-up radio or doing a first aid course. The important thing is that you start and that you do a little towards your plan whenever you can. And remember – knowledge and planning are far more powerful than any survival gadget you may spot on the internet.

# Medical Care During SHTF

If there is one thing many preppers do wrong, it is not having a decent first aid kit. Most opt for a $30 kit from the drug store or department store and think that is sufficient. It isn't. Not when you are thinking of an SHTF survival scenario, in any case.

The only way to ensure that you have what you need is to buy a full trauma kit or make your own. For survival purposes, your first aid kit has to have two things: depth and breadth – and shop-bought kits don't offer either.

What does that mean, depth and breadth? Starting with the latter, breadth means having the right gear to treat many different injuries, from minor to serious trauma injuries; for depth, it means having enough in a kit to deal with several different serious injuries.

You need to keep in mind that medical facilities are likely to become overcrowded and unable to function properly. You may not even be able to get to a hospital or clinic, and having that full trauma kit may well save a life or two.

The most important thing to remember is that first aid is only that, and unless you are a surgeon or a trained paramedic, all you can do with serious injuries is to stop them from getting worse. And some medical supplies, in the wrong untrained hands, can do more harm than good. That is why you should never attempt any kind of assistance that you are not trained for.

### Your Kit

The obvious place to start is with your kit bag. It must be something that your kit can be properly organized in, perhaps a case with several divided sections or compartments. A big fishing tackle box is ideal because there are plenty of organizational spaces for small and large items.

Next comes the contents of your kit, and it is recommended to avoid cheap supplies; go for high-quality medical supplies because it can make all the difference when you need to treat someone.

### Hygiene

This is one of the most important things to remember - many wounds are not likely to kill anyone unless a major organ has been damaged. Typically, people die from wounds if they bleed out or if the wound has become infected, and while a bandage may stop bleeding, it won't stop an infection. This is why wounds and the area around them must be kept clean, and that means stopping yourself from adding bacteria. Make sure you are clean before you attempt to clean a wound and make sure you are protected from any infections disease the person has.

- **Antibacterial hand sanitizer** - wash your hands before you touch a wound
- **Sterile gloves** - they must be sterile, and you must put them on before you treat anyone
- **Medical face mask** - to stop you breathing germs into a wound
- **CPR mask** - protects you and the person from infection should CPR be required

**Flesh Wounds**

These are what most of your first aid kit is going to treat, and it could be something minor, such as a cut, to a severed limb. Your goal is to stop it bleeding and provide the wound with protection. The size and severity of the wound will determine what you do.

- **Irrigation Syringe** – to clean the wound before bandaging it. Squirt clean drinking water into the wound
- **Alcohol wipes** – to clean the wound and the surrounding area (you'll need a large supply of these)
- **Antibacterial ointment** – for putting on the wound to prevent bacteria causing infection
- **Steri-Strips/butterfly closures** – used for closing open or separated wounds to protect them, to slow or stop bleeding, and encourage healing
- **Clotting agent** – something like QuickClot or Celox, designed to help clot blood. Some bandages are fused with it, or you can buy crystals
- **Cloth adhesive bandage strips** – flexible, so they don't come off so easily
- **Knuckle bandages** – not the easiest thing to bandage but these work by keeping things clean and moving with the fingers
- **Fingertip bandages** – another tough area to bandage
- **Large bandages** – sterile gauze pads; keep a variety of different sizes for different sized wounds. These do not contain any adhesive
- **Medical tape** – to keep the bandages in place
- **SWAT-Tourniquet** – great as a tourniquet, but when half-tightened, they act as a pressure dressing to reduce bleeding

- **Israeli Bandage** – a combat bandage with a clotting agent and a wrap to hold it in place; it can also be used as a pressure dressing

**Broken Bones**

These are typically fractures or compound fractures, the latter of which is identified by the bone protruding through the skin. In these cases, both the fracture and the wound must be treated, while with a simple fracture, only the bone must be treated.

- **Splints** – you can use almost anything as a splint, but a SAM splint is one of the easiest; constructed of soft aluminum and foam rubber, it can be cut to size and is malleable
- **Elastic bandages** – you might know them as Ace bandages, required to hold the splint in place, treat sprains, and ligament injuries
- **Combat cravat** – another bandage; triangular in shape and used for making slings

**Must-Have Medical Tools**

As well as medical supplies, you need tools for both simple and serious injuries. Even if you are not trained in using medical tools, these can make all the difference:

- **Medical Scissors** – to cut bandages and clothing off (make sure you get a good pair)
- **Fine-pointed tweezers** – to remove gravel and splinters
- **Jewelers Loupe** – a small magnifying glass that the eye socket holds in place – useful for finding fine splinters, thorns, and so on
- **Hemostats** – should you have to work with a severed limb, these close off veins to stop blood pumping out
- **Tourniquet** – the one-handed type is best, just in case you need it on yourself
- **Stethoscope** – not an absolute must

- **Blood pressure monitor** – when blood pressure drops, it could signal internal bleeding
- **Blood sugar monitor** – self-explanatory: use it on people who are shaky, are not thinking clearly, suddenly lose strength, or feel as if they're going to faint
- **Thermometer** – an increase in temperature indicates fever and potential infection. In-ear thermometers are the best ones or the forehead strip type
- **Eyecup** – for cleaning eyes, used with saline or sterile water

## Other Things You Need in Your SHTF Kit

There are so many things you could put in your kit that the big question is: Where do you stop? You can go as far as you want, but these are the must-haves:

- **Instant ice packs** – good for sprains or any non-bleeding injury to reduce swelling; you can also use ice spray
- **Tegaderm** – a film dressing for use over burns and rashes to hold the medical cream in place
- **Benzoin** – used for cleaning areas around wounds to ensure the bandage will stick
- **Lidocaine** – local anesthetic: injection or topical use for reducing pain in wounds
- **Anti-inflammatory medication** – things like ibuprofen or diclotard, anything like that will do the trick

## Tips for Treating Wounds

Try to get into the frame of mind where you treat all wounds AS IF they were life-threatening. A mnemonic, ASIF helps you to memorize basic treatment for wounds and lacerations:

### A = Amount of Bleeding

Is it a venous or arterial wound? Arterial blood is brighter and streaming or pulsing out. It must be stopped with a tourniquet or compression bandage. If you don't have one, create one by placing a sterile gauze over the wound and apply some pressure – if the person can help, get them to apply the pressure. Elevate the wound if you can and wrap an elastic bandage around it – start from where the wound is closer to the toes or fingers (distal) and work toward the heart (proximal). This will stop blood pooling in the patient's extremities. Do not wrap the bandage tighter to get more pressure – turn it a half-turn, wrapping it over itself, over the wound, and continue to wrap.

### S = Shock

Many injuries create shock, even psychogenic shock at times. Reassure the person, keep them warm and calm, and as comfortable as you can. Never say anything meaningless, such as "It's going to be all right." Be supportive and strong; the more you can reassure the person that you are helping them, the more their body will focus on healing without stress, adrenaline, and other factors that can knock off the physiology of balance.

### I = Irrigate

If the wound is not arterial or life-threatening, and you can get into it, clean it out. There are plenty of germs just waiting to get into it, so clean as quickly and thoroughly as possible.

### F = Functional/Further Damage

If you can clean the wound, inspect it to see if there is any functional damage. Have any major vessels, tendons, or nerves been severed? Can the person move their fingers or toes? If there is any damage, you need to treat that too. If, for example, an extensor tendon has been severed, surgery is required to heal it. You cannot do that. If it was just nicked, you must stop the person from extending the specific digit so it can heal.

### Stitches

Many people think they can stitch a wound, but in primitive, remote, or post-disaster environments, stitching a wound is irresponsible. In many simple wounds, suturing is not necessary and can cause infection. Use your bandages to keep the wound clean, but leave it to heal on its own. Use Steri-Strips if you can, and tight bandaging is okay for some wounds. Unless you are medically qualified to do it, steer clear of suturing.

### Infection

This is likely to be the biggest issue you will face in post-disaster scenarios. Treating an infection is easier if you can catch it early enough, and that means knowing what signs to look out for. Every wound will show inflammation to a certain degree, and there will almost always be some infection. Some of the key points to look for are:

- **Redness** – inflammation causes a certain amount of redness, but infection creates a whole lot more because more of the tissues are inflamed. It will often be a much brighter shade of red too
- **Swelling** – again, inflammation causes some swelling, but the swelling caused by an infection is typically down to pus, and if touched, causes sharp pain. These usually drain by themselves
- **Pain** – inflammation causes more of an ache, but infection causes sharper pains. This is typical of infection if it hurts while that part of the body is being rested or a much sharper pain is felt when moving after being still for a while. Pain caused by infection could be local to one area, or it may be more spread out than inflammation pain, which tends to be only around the wound area
- **Pus** – otherwise called exudate, pus indicates an infection and not inflammation
- **Fever** – this is one of the more serious indicators that infection is present and has gone further than you want it to be in a post-disaster scenario

- **Streaking** – if you see red streaks following the veins, it signals a serious infection

### How to Deal with Infection

Typically, infections are treated with antibiotics, but you may not have any on hand, or you may not have the correct type. What if you give antibiotics and the infection doesn't respond? Or, as is the most common case, you may not have the expertise and training to know whether an antibiotic is working or not, or whether the person has an allergic reaction to it.

No matter which perspective you come from, the first thing is to clean the wound. If infection sets in within the damaged tissues, again, clean it thoroughly. Activated charcoal is one of the best ways, not to mention the most efficient, for cleaning infected wounds, and you can buy it in tablet, capsule, or loose powder form.

### Using Charcoal

Using clean drinking water (distilled is best), add it to the charcoal to make a paste – tablets may be crushed and capsules opened and emptied. Charcoal bonds weakly to water, and when used in a wound, it will pick up anything it comes into contact with. Basically, charcoal is a micro-sponge, cleaning and absorbing bacteria, toxins, and dead tissues that feed bacteria.

Once you have mixed it, apply it into the wound and around it. Put a gauze pad over the top and secure it in place in whatever manner works. Within a few hours, you should start to see changes in the state of the tissue. Change the charcoal mixture every few hours until the tissue is no longer carrying an infection.

One thing you must understand is that skills and knowledge are more important than having the biggest survival first aid kit. It does not matter what is in your kit – it is knowing how to use it correctly that counts. Every person in your prepper team should attend a first aid course and keep their training current too. And you should always have an up-to-date first aid booklet in your kit as well.

# Additional First Aid Checklist

Combine this list with the previous one given to you:

- Antibacterial hand sanitizer
- Sterile gloves
- Medical face mask
- CPR mask
- Irrigation syringe
- Alcohol wipes
- Antibacterial ointment
- Steri-Strips/butterfly closures
- Clotting agent – QuickClot or Celox, etc.
- Cloth adhesive bandage strips
- Knuckle bandages
- Fingertip bandages
- Large bandages
- Medical tape
- SWAT-Tourniquet
- Israeli Bandage
- Splints
- Elastic bandages
- Combat cravat

- Medical scissors
- Fine-pointed tweezers
- Loupe
- Hemostats
- Tourniquet
- Stethoscope
- Blood pressure monitor
- Blood sugar monitor
- Thermometer
- Eyecup
- Instant ice packs
- Tegaderm
- Benzoin
- Lidocaine
- Anti-inflammatory medication
- Charcoal powder, capsule or tablet

# The Bug-out Bag: Surviving SHTF On the Go

The BOB – your bug-out bag – is an essential part of prepping for an SHTF scenario, and it is nothing more than a kit that you can grab and go. It is an all-in-one emergency survival kit, and every member of your prepper family must have one, even your dog. The bug-out bag is designed to be carried and keep you alive for at least three days following an SHTF disaster, but for it to do that, it needs a few essential items.

Do this right, and while everyone else is panicking, running around like headless chickens, you will be way ahead of them and able to sleep, provide for you and your family (with safety, food, water, the means to hunt), wash, and communicate. It all comes down to what you put in your bug-out bags and how prepared you are.

If you are new to prepping, you might be a little overwhelmed by the bug-out bag, especially as you need more than one – one for each member of your group and at least one spare in the car. And if you have a bug-out shelter somewhere, put another one there too – it can be the difference between life and death.

Most preppers continually tweak their bags to make sure they have got everything they need. The hard part is knowing where to start, so here are the seven basic types of gear you need in your bag – once you have these, you can tweak them to your heart's content:

### 1. Water

Water is a basic survival requirement. You can only go three days without it, and when the SHTF, it soon becomes one of the most valuable commodities.

As a bare minimum, you need one liter per person per day – aiming for a minimum of three days, each bag needs at least three liters of water. You will also need a water purification system to purify other sources of water you come across. It can be a small camp kettle and some iodine tablets or a full-on water filter. Have a collapsible backpacking bucket so you can easily collect more water, and a pack or two of coffee filters to make your filtration system last longer.

### 2. Food

For a three-day BOB, you can get by on energy bars and freeze-dried meals – these need boiling water. These products don't weigh anything and last for ages. In the long term, your bug-out shelter will need a larger supply of food.

### 3. Clothing

The clothes in your bag should be no different from what you would need for a weekend hiking/backpacking break:

- Sturdy shoes or boots
- Long pants (not jeans)
- Two pairs of socks (not cotton)
- Two shirts – one long, one short-sleeved
- A warm waterproof jacket
- Long warm underwear
- A hat
- A bandana

This list could go on, and many preppers pack at least twice the amount of clothes – this list should see you through the first three days, though. One thing you must do is pack according to the weather.

### 4. Shelter

For three days bugging out, you need shelter and somewhere dry and warm to sleep:

- A tent or a tarp you can set up
- A ground tarp and a sleeping pad
- A bedroll or good sleeping bag

If you opt for a tarp instead of a tent, make sure you take whatever you need to set it up.

### 5. First Aid Kit

As mentioned earlier, what you need as an absolute minimum in your bug-out bag is a first aid kit. It's recommended that you make your kit – don't just buy one off the shelf and think it will be enough. Best case, the contents will be cheap, and worst case, you won't have what you need, but you will have a load of stuff you won't need.

Building your own familiarizes you with the kit and how to use it too, which is essential when you are bugging out.

### 6. Basic Gear

These are the things you cannot do without but don't fall into any other category. You do not have to follow this list exactly, just use it as an idea of what you should have.

- A minimum of two ways to shelter from the rain – a poncho, coat, tent, etc.
- At least three ways of starting a fire
- Something for chopping firewood
- A small backpack stove, fuel, and something for boiling water for your meals

- A minimum of two good flashlights and plenty of extra batteries
- A survival knife

There are other things, and this guide detailed earlier what you should have in your bug-out bag.

## 7. Weapons

You may find yourself in a lawless situation, and in times of desperation, people do desperate things. Expect the worst, and make sure you are well prepared for defending yourself and your family. You should have a firearm of some kind, whatever you are comfortable using – and one that you have had some training and practice in using too. Don't turn vigilante, though; only use the gun if it is absolutely necessary.

You can also use your survival knife as a weapon if you need to, and even carrying a club or a large walking stick can be a deterrent. The long and the short of it is: Have several defense options and be prepared to use them in a desperate situation.

To finish off, you are going to look at some basic wilderness survival tips.

# Wilderness Survival Tips

The wilderness is a tough place to be for a day, let alone for days, weeks, potentially months on end. Your mental and physical strength will be tested to their limits, and it really is a case of survival of the fittest. Most people think that they could survive in the wilderness easily, but what would you do in the event of an accident? How will you really cope? And are there any tips or tricks that could help you?

Here are six basic steps you should learn, master, and remember if you are to survive in the wilderness:

### 1. Have the Right State of Mind

In other words, get a grip. Your state of mind is the key to your survival – if you are prone to panic, you won't last long. Panic equals bad decisions, without thinking about the consequences; if you start making impulsive choices, you are minimizing your chances of survival and rescue.

Even if a fast decision is needed, take a minute (or a few moments if the decision is imminent) to relax. You will make much better decisions and find more efficient solutions. While cortisol and adrenaline help you, do some deep breathing to bring your blood pressure down. Inhale for a count of five, exhale for a count of four, slowly. Repeat until you are under control.

## 2. Always Have a Plan

Start with what is the most important and work from there. For example, if someone has injured themselves, that must be dealt with before anything else - that's where your first aid kit comes in, along with knowledge on dealing with common injuries.

Once that has been dealt with, you and your entire group need to decide who is doing what and how the chores are going to be divided. You also need to decide how long to stay in one place and when to move on.

If you have gotten lost, you should sit tight to make it easier for rescue. If you have a good survival watch, you can get yourself out of trouble - they have compasses, barometers, altimeters, and more on them, ensuring you know what's coming and where to go.

If you opt to move on, you need a plan for shelter, water, and food.

## 3. Build a Shelter

This is one of the first things you should do when out in the wilderness. If you have your bug-out bag, you should have shelter and a sleeping bag, but if you don't, you're going to have to build one, especially if the night is drawing near.

Find a large fallen log and lift it to lean against a rock or another large tree. That's your shelter foundation. Cover it with branches, leaves, and brush, and if you have one, spread a tarp over the top to keep the rain out.

Clear bugs and sharp rocks from the ground and make a bed from leaves and twigs. If you are caught out in heavy snow, dig a hole and spend the night there - do make sure the entrance can't get blocked by drifting snow or an avalanche, though. Small caves are also ideal shelters, especially as you can build a fire in the entrance. Do make sure no animals inhabit the cave before you move in, though.

Avoid crevices, anywhere that can potentially flood or anywhere that might be home to large wild animals.

### 4. Make a Fire

This is the next important thing and easily done if you have waterproof matches. Light a bunch of twigs, and keep adding larger branches. Make sure all the wood is dry, or the fire will struggle to light and stay alight.

If you do not have any matches, use friction to create a spark - build a nest from dry leaves and grass, then find a piece of flat wood. Make a small notch in the wood. Put a piece of bark under the notch, and using a pointed twig or small piece of wood, spin it first in the hole, rolling it until embers light the board. Then you can transfer this to the bark and start your fire in your nest.

If the sun is high and strong, and you have glasses, use them to direct the sun at the nest; it will catch fire. The same can be done with a plastic bottle.

### 5. Find Food and Water

If you don't have your bug-out bag with you, you will need food and water, particularly the latter. If you are carrying a water purifier and have a water source nearby, you have a great source of water. If not, produce your own by collecting rainfall from leaves. You could wrap green branches with plastic bags and wait for them to sweat too.

For food, if you have any with you, ration it. If not, find food. You can set traps or hunt for animals if you have the tools with you, or look for insects, such as larvae, worms, and other small bugs - these are packed with protein, and you'll find them in humid dark places under rocks, and around trees.

Do make sure you know the difference between poisonous and safe insects and plants.

### 6. Signal for Some Help

To do this, use all that you have on hand three times – a whistle should be blown three times, with a few seconds break, and then again.

Build three campfires; if you are moving, tie ribbons on three trees in a group, or leave three rock mounds.

If you have a satellite phone, you are in a good position to get help by sending an alert message.

The last tip: Whenever you leave for the wilderness, make sure someone knows where you are and what your itinerary is.

# Conclusion

Congratulations on making it to the end of this guide. This book should have been useful and provided you with all of the information you need regarding prepping for survival. As you can see, you cannot learn to prep overnight. It is not a hobby; it is a serious business, and one everyone should be learning right now.

It isn't about buying up your entire supermarket and filling fridges, freezers, and cupboards with loads of food, just in case. It isn't about buying up your local camping store, just in case. It is about stockpiling the right stuff in the right quantities. It's about learning new skills that will help you survive in a worst-case scenario. It's about being prepared for whatever happens without being reckless about it.

Why fill your fridge and freezer when the first thing that is likely to go is your electricity supply? Why spend hours making your garden look pretty with flowers when you should be growing food that will keep? Why look at life with an "it will never happen to me" attitude – millions of people the world over have thought that way and millions of people have gotten caught out.

Read and learn because, one day, the S really will HTF – will you be prepared?

# References

https://www.youtube.com/watch?v=WLa0RRU0-G8

https://www.youtube.com/watch?v=7AUiV2zorwg

https://www.youtube.com/watch?v=E459XIluUFE

https://www.survivalsullivan.com/16-surprising-benefits-of-prepping/

https://www.youtube.com/watch?v=o9niShq9_Dg

https://www.askaprepper.com/24-prepping-items-dont-spend-money/

https://www.youtube.com/watch?v=1j5V4rJ2g5I

https://www.youtube.com/watch?v=VtcDiyj9T8k

https://www.happypreppers.com/skills.html

https://www.youtube.com/watch?v=byKqaGUiaFM

https://www.youtube.com/watch?v=Ln5qRknownw

https://www.mnn.com/lifestyle/responsible-living/stories/going-off-the-grid-why-more-people-are-choosing-to-live-life-un

https://www.youtube.com/watch?v=v8Pe_u_4q5M

https://www.youtube.com/watch?v=09IK9OvWpjw

https://www.youtube.com/watch?v=4ts15BW-6hw

https://www.youtube.com/watch?v=8-86NFf2VcE

https://thetinylife.com/common-off-grid-living-misconceptions/

https://morningchores.com/homesteading/

http://www.therealfarmhouse.com/10-steps-to-start-homesteading-on-the-cheap/

https://www.offthegridnews.com/how-to-2/9-crucial-steps-for-the-first-time-homesteader/

https://www.youtube.com/watch?v=fFHn_xoMsAs

https://www.youtube.com/watch?v=w4qcoEXYqK0

https://rurallivingtoday.com/homesteading-today/realistic-off-grid-power-sources/ https://www.treehugger.com/sustainable-product-design/generating-off-grid-power-the-four-best-ways.html

https://insteading.com/blog/off-grid-water-system/

https://www.youtube.com/watch?v=bBF72Een1D8

https://offgridworld.com/how-much-does-it-really-cost-to-go-off-grid/

https://www.youtube.com/watch?v=hJpwy9mUmho

https://www.youtube.com/watch?v=Aa74smEC0OM

https://www.youtube.com/watch?v=vDQUEuTL8tk

https://www.youtube.com/watch?v=K4wO76cqkOU

https://www.skilledsurvival.com/build-survival-medical-kit-scratch/

https://www.youtube.com/watch?v=ks00XG3n7yM

https://survivalistprepper.net/shtf-injuries-and-prevention-for-preppers/

https://unchartedsupplyco.com/blogs/news/bug-out-bag-checklist

https://www.youtube.com/watch?v=ToonXShDAFk

https://www.youtube.com/watch?v=stIjgEaES60

https://www.oldfashionedfamilies.com/6-misconceptions-about-preppers/

https://thepreppingguide.com/what-is-prepping/

https://www.shtfpreparedness.com/new-prepping-start/

https://www.askaprepper.com/24-prepping-items-dont-spend-money/

www.ingramcontent.com/pod-product-compliance
Lightning Source LLC
Chambersburg PA
CBHW070047230426
43661CB00005B/800